MYSTERY MAGIC
&
MIRACLE

Religion in a Post=Aquarian Age

edited by
Edward F. Heenan

D1475216

A SPECTRUM BOOK

PRENTICE-HALL, INC., ENGLEWOOD CLIFFS, N.J.

Library of Congress Cataloging in Publication Data

HEENAN, EDWARD F   comp.
   Mystery, magic & miracle.

   (A Spectrum Book)
   Includes bibliographical references.
      1. United States—Religion.   I. Title.
BR526.H35   200'.973   73–932
ISBN 0–13–609032–X
ISBN 0–13–609024–9 (pbk)

Cover Credit: Alinari–Art Reference Bureau:
The Ecstasy of St. Teresa, by Bernini

10   9   8   7   6   5   4   3   2   1

PRENTICE-HALL INTERNATIONAL, INC. (*London*)
PRENTICE-HALL OF AUSTRALIA PTY. LTD. (*Sydney*)
PRENTICE-HALL OF CANADA LTD. (*Toronto*)
PRENTICE-HALL OF INDIA PRIVATE LIMITED (*New Delhi*)
PRENTICE-HALL OF JAPAN, INC. (*Tokyo*)

CONTENTS

PREFACE

This book is about religion in the post-Aquarian Age. It draws together works by participants in and observers of psychedelic drugs,
the occult, and the Jesus movement that describe and explain the
current religious revival in the youth culture. In focusing on the mysterious, magical, and miraculous aspects of the religious revival, it is
hoped that a better understanding of what is happening both in and
to religion in America will be achieved.

Although I am not a believer in witchcraft, I am grateful to both
Herbert Sloane and Roberta Kennedy, two sincere believers who
were kind enough to share some of their beliefs with me. Andrew
Getsinger and Linda Okapal deserve my thanks for their persistence
in gathering the materials used in this book. I also would like to
thank Betty Greene and Eleanor Champagne for their devotion to
the task of typing and editing the manuscript. Finally, I would like
to express my deepest appreciation to Harriet R. Falkenstein for her
comments on earlier drafts of the manuscript.

For My Mother and Father

ACKNOWLEDGMENTS

We gratefully acknowledge the following for their permission to reprint lyrics appearing in this volume:

All selections from the rock opera TOMMY, by The Who, Copyrighted © 1969 by Fabulous Music Ltd. Reprinted by permission of Track Music, Inc. All rights reserved. Reproduction prohibited.

All selections from HAIR, Copyright © 1966, 1967, 1968. Proprietors James Rado, Gerome Ragni, Galt MacDermot, Nat Shapiro, and United Artists Music Company, Inc. All rights controlled and administered by United Artists Music Company, Inc., 729 Seventh Avenue, New York, N.Y. 10019.

INTRODUCTION:
THE SECOND REFORMATION

Edward F. Heenan

When Martin Luther fastened his ninety-five theses to the door of All Saints' Church on the eve of All Saints' Day in 1517, he initiated a religious revolution in Christianity whose impact has lasted for over four hundred years. From that point in history the unity of Western religion was lost in the rise of Protestantism. Perhaps even more important than the dissolution of religious unity was the inherent rejection in Protestantism of the mysterious, magical, and miraculous phenomena that had been endemic to the Catholic tradition.[1] The effect was to place ecstasy, charismatic gifts, mysticism, and emotionalism outside mainstream Protestantism and into the sphere of religious minority groups.[2] Since Protestantism became the dominant religion early in American history, religion in the United States has become increasingly rationalistic, bureaucratic, and pragmatic.

When Timothy Leary organized the League for Spiritual Discovery in Millbrook, New York, in the late 1960s, he gave impetus to a second religious revolution in Christianity, the impact of which has yet to be fully felt. From that point in history, it became clear that a significant number of American youth had rediscovered the values of mystery, magic, and miracle in their quest for meaningful definitions of society and self. They had become disenchanted with many of the institutional aspects of the traditional church, the roots of which can be traced back to the first Reformation. Instead of simple adherence to systems of belief, they sought profound religious experience. In effect, these young Americans have created the seeds of a second Reformation.

1. Peter L. Berger, *The Sacred Canopy: Elements of a Sociological Theory of Religion* (Garden City, New York: Doubleday and Company, Inc., 1967), p. 111.

2. H. Richard Niebuhr, *The Social Sources of Denominationalism* (New York: Meridian Books, Inc., 1957).

In religion man feels that he is in contact with a transcendent reality, the power of which has created and continues to support his being. Mystery, magic, and miracle must, therefore, be considered integral parts of religion since they are identified with a transcendent reality that gives ultimate meaning to life. However, they have come to be identified in Western culture with antiscientific or superstitious beliefs. What is more, magic has acquired a sinister significance because of its association with witchcraft and the "black arts." Thus, while mystery, magic, and miracle cannot be divorced from religion in that they are a part of the Christian tradition, they have come to mean something different from what is commonly understood by the term *religion*. Through mystery, magic, and miracle it is felt that man is attempting to contact occult forces and not, as is the case in religion, sacred powers in the perennial struggle between good and evil.

Sociologists of religion, with a few notable exceptions, have been concerned with religion in its organizational context.[3] That is, they have been concerned more with the rational aspects of religion than the irrational, the bureaucratic more than the ecstatic, and the pragmatic more than the transcendent.

The reason for this apparent uninterest in the mysterious, magical, and miraculous aspects of religion is threefold. First, the liberal strains in American theology have moved away from the supernatural and the transcendent. Mystery, magic, and miracle are therefore less frequently present in institutional religion, and are thus likely to be overlooked by the sociologists of religion. Second, sociologists of religion lack the methodological tools to study religious experience; they simply are not equipped to handle the irrational, the ecstatic, or the transcendent. Third, religionists have long had a deep distrust of the social scientist. They feel he is incapable of understanding the true dimensions of religion as they see it. As a consequence, sociologists of religion, as well as theologians, have fostered a schizophrenia in American religion between transcendent and institutional aspects of religion. Their biases against and limitations in handling the supernatural have, to a remarkable degree, influenced what they have looked at and what they have avoided.

Early in the last decade they told us God had just died, although Jesus was still mentioned in public—but not with reverence. Scholars

3. For example, see: Andrew M. Greeley, "Implications for the Sociology of Religion of Occult Behavior in the Youth Culture," in *Youth and Society*, 2 (1970), 131–40; Andrew M. Greeley, "There's a New Time Religion on Campus," in *The New York Times Magazine*, June 1, 1969, pp. 14ff.; and Marcello Truzzi, "The Occult Revival as Popular Culture: Some Random Observations on the Old and Nouveau Witch," in *Sociological Quarterly*, 13, no. 1 (1972), 16–36.

were defensive about religion as an intellectual pursuit, and clergymen were bewildered and attempting to adapt to change in the most improbable ways. Laymen were smug and lethargic, and young people were "turned off" by the church. The spotlight quickly shifted to civil rights, the peace movement, the zero population movement, and all the other popular movements that occupied the interests of social scientists in the latter half of the 1960s.

Yet while religion appeared to have lost its importance, it is not true that nothing was happening in the church during the last decade. First, sociologists of religion noted that churches either found, or continued to employ, a formula for survival. Institutions die hard and the churches have experienced only slight attrition in membership and attendance. This does not startle us now, but only a few years ago many social scientists whose credentials are honorable were predicting the quick demise of organized religion in the United States.

Second, most of the research indicates that the churches became more fundamentalist and that those churches that were already fundamentalist grew at a disproportionate pace.[4] This is explained both by their recruitment and retention practices and by the fact that "denomination switchers" tend to move toward increasingly liberal denominations until they achieve a private noninstitutionalized religion. This process leaves the institutional church to those who will support it with their time and money—that is, fundamentalists.

Third, social scientists showed that the age of ecumenism never really developed. To be sure, there were mergers, but they were more easily explained by economics than theology. A form of ecumenism did, however, occur. For example, a liberal Lutheran realized that his religious beliefs and opinions were closer to those of a liberal Presbyterian than to those of a fundamentalist Lutheran in his own congregation. Conversely, the conflict over religious issues was more evident within churches than between them.

Fourth, researchers noted that the Vietnam War legitimized radical pacifism as an ideological posture in American religion.[5] It became possible for denominations other than Quaker to be both religious and pacifist. Similarly, disillusionment with denominational alignments generated the tendency to form private religious ties with issue-oriented groups. These issue-oriented groups formed an underground church that represented a new style of ecumenism.

4. Rodney Stark and Charles Y. Glock, *American Piety: The Nature of Religious Commitment* (Berkeley: University of California Press, 1968), pp. 183–221.

5. Richard J. Neuhaus, "The War, the Churches, and Civil Religion," in *Annals of the American Academy of Political and Social Science*, 387 (1970), 128–40.

Fifth, social scientists observed the development of multiple images among the clergy. At the national level, the 10 percent who actively engaged in dissent over the Vietnam War were perhaps the conscience of the nation—an image that was especially attractive to nonbelievers. Fundamentalist laity gravitated to a pietistic and administrative clergy, while liberals idolized charisma and relevance. Each group ruled out the opposing image as illegitimate.

Finally, research indicates that the churches continued to bureaucratize and were beginning to awaken to a sense of corporate power. For instance, many of them began to scrutinize their investment portfolios. They quickly recognized that it was somewhat difficult to account for the discrepancy between the protests of their members against American corporate involvement in Southeast Asia and the fact that the corporate church benefited from this involvement.

As a result of their research, social scientists suggested that the divisions within the church in the '60s were leading it to the brink of a civil war. Protestantism was preparing for a palace revolt stemming from the structural and ideological schism between clergy and laity. The clergy were significantly more liberal on all social issues than the laity.[6] They were living in different worlds, perceiving different realities, and coming dangerously close to forming two churches in one organizational setting. In Catholicism, on the other hand, the war was shaping up as a revolt of the masses, with the lowerarchy (lower clergy and laity) pitted against the hierarchy.[7]

However, the civil war in organized religion simply did not occur in the 1970s as anticipated. While social scientists were looking at the churches in the hopes of documenting the revolution they foresaw, they missed the actual spiritual revolution that had begun in the United States. This revolution has been primarily concerned with the resurgence of mystery, magic, and miracle and has occurred outside the church in such places as the drug scene, the occult explosion, and the Jesus movement.

These three phenomena shed light on some of the areas of transcendence that have been largely ignored by social scientists. The ethos of the drug scene is basic to understanding religion in a post-Aquarian age because psychedelic drugs have reawakened a dormant interest in the mysterious and transcendent aspects of religion. Specifically, psychedelic

6. Jeffrey K. Hadden, *The Gathering Storm in the Churches* (Garden City, New York: Doubleday and Company, Inc., 1969); Phillip E. Hammond and Robert E. Mitchell, "Segmentation of Radicalism—The Case of the Protestant Campus Ministers," in *American Journal of Sociology*, 71, no. 2 (1965), 133–43.

7. Joseph H. Fichter, *America's Forgotten Priests: What They Are Saying* (New York: Harper and Row, Publishers, Inc., 1968).

drugs can offer mystical phenomena on a scale never before possible in the history of religion. That is, psychedelic drugs can induce religious experiences in mass society, and, what is more, it can be done without a formally organized church. In addition, the drug ethos has permeated society and expanded the interest in transcendent experience to such an extent that it made possible the emergence of both the occult explosion and the Jesus movement. The occult explosion is best seen as the resurgence of the magical aspects of religion that had been eliminated in the dominance of Protestantism. That is, the occult, at its most serious level, is essentially a religious movement concerned with the two elements common to each of the religious phenomena of the post-Aquarian age, transcendence and the supernatural. The Jesus movement is an attempt to revitalize Christianity by returning to some of the miraculous aspects of religion; it is a religious phenomenon whose focal point is the miraculous and the transcendent.

While mystery may be associated primarily with psychedelics, magic with the occult, and miracle with the Jesus movement, there are several basic commonalities among these phenomena. They are characteristically emotional, personalized, enthusiastic, antirational, antireason, and youth oriented. They are the last sphere of American life to be discovered by the youth culture, and like the youth culture itself, they stand at the fringe of our culture poised either for cooptation by or humanization of the culture.

THE EMERGING FORMS OF RELIGION IN THE 1970s

The question that demands an answer now is why the emphasis of religious expression in the late 1960s and early 1970s changed from rationalism, bureaucracy, and pragmatism to mystery, magic, and miracle.

Social scientists have usually explained the renewed interest in these supernatural aspects of religion as a reaction either to hyper-rationalism —to the impersonal nature of bureaucratized society—or to the glorification of science. Other conditions, such as the transitory nature of human relationships and the secularization of the churches, have also been offered as explanations for the resurgence of mystery, magic, and miracle, but they are inadequate because they do not tell us why this resurgence has occurred at this particular time. Such explanations apply to all forms of social change without differentiating either the level or the intensity of such change. Nevertheless, they do affirm the importance of religious experience, whereas only ten years ago few social scientists thought it important enough even to comment on.

To understand and explain the emerging forms of religion, one must comprehend the impact of (1) the larger cultural context of religion, (2) the changes in America's civil religion, and (3) the relationship of the youth culture to religion.

The Cultural Context

Western culture underwent a radical change either after or during the historical period in which most of the now-established religions were founded. Between the 16th and 18th centuries the Western world became qualitatively different because of the combined quantitative impact of four variables: population, organization, environmental resources, and scientific technology.[8] The result of the quantum leap in the nature of these variables was that the value system, both religious and secular, of contemporary society has been imbalanced, causing traditional and emerging systems to exist side by side. Let us review briefly the changes in these variables and their impact on religion.

Man, in the millenia of his existence on this planet, produced only 500 million persons simultaneously alive by the mid-17th century. By 1970, the population exceeded 3.6 billion. In the United States, the population growth was also staggering. When the first census was taken in 1790 there were only 4 million Americans. In 1970 there were more than 200 million—an increase of about 45 times. But in addition to its sheer size the population has become increasingly more dense in recent history. In 1790 there were only twenty-four cities and towns, most with populations below 5,000. In 1970, there were about twenty-five cities of a million or more inhabitants. Finally, this shift in population also correlates with other social variables. If you are poor, a member of a minority group, handicapped, or old, you are more likely to be part of the population that lives closer to the inner city. Population increase and changes in the patterns of distribution have provided the raw material for changes in our culture.

These population changes resulted in several religious changes. The churches in the 1950s experienced an unprecedented growth in membership as a result of the population shift from cities to the suburbs —which necessitated the building of new churches to accommodate the increasing demand of new residents for religious organizations in their communities. During this period, the older churches, located primarily in the cities, were called upon to support the establishment of these new suburban churches.

The dramatic increase in population and the events of the Industrial Revolution encouraged the growth of larger and more complex organizations while they destroyed the viability of others. At about this

8. For further information about these variables see Philip M. Hauser and Leo F. Schnore, eds., *The Study of Urbanization* (New York: John Wiley and Sons, Inc., 1965).

time the Western world adopted bureaucracy as the major form of complex organization. Yet although bureaucracies were developed to organize large groups of people, it was never certain that they could accommodate an infinite number without showing signs of strain and collapse or, at least, an inability to meet the needs for which they were designed. This inadequacy has recently manifested itself in all bureaucracies, from the churches to the federal government. As a rough indicator of the increasing size and complexity of bureaucracies in the recent past, consider that in 1790 there were only one thousand civilian employees of the federal government. By 1960 the number had risen to 2.5 million. At present, bureaucracies are manifesting some of the pathologies common to a form of human organization which is overtaxed.

In order to manage the growth in size of their congregations, the churches were forced to bureaucratize. In adapting to population changes through organizational means, other problems arose, involving conflict over social cleavages in the congregations, community issues, religious values and beliefs, and the role of the minister.

The increasing scale of Western culture is also exemplified by the use of our environmental resources. Isaac Asimov estimates that we are extracting 20 billion billion calories of energy from our environment each year. In 1902, for instance, the kilowatt hours of electricity produced was 5,965 million; by 1957, it had risen to 716,000 million. The trend in the use of the environment is summarized well by Dr. Homi Bhabha:

". . . let us use the letter 'Q' to stand for the energy derived from burning some 33,000 million tons of coal. In the eighteen and one half centuries after Christ, the total energy consumed averaged less than one half Q per century. But by 1850, the rate had risen to one Q per century." This means, roughly speaking, that half of all the energy consumed by man in the past 2,000 years has been consumed in the last one hundred.[9]

Only quite recently has it been realized that the resources of the earth are finite. The contemporary equation between the depletion of resources and the accretion of the wastes of these resources has been recognized; as one grows smaller, the other gets larger.

The effect of the changing environment on the churches has been to awaken in religious institutions a sense of their responsibility to protect the environment. The early Judeo-Christian tradition as articulated in the Book of Genesis legitimized the dominance of man over his environment. However, with the first Reformation and resulting in-

9. Quoted in Alvin Toffler, *Future Shock* (New York: Bantam Books, Inc., 1970), p. 23.

dustrialization, this early ideology got out of hand. The Protestant ethic alienated man from nature; the environment was desacralized—it became something to be owned and exploited by the individual. In the process man changed from "homo sapiens" to "homo polluticus." The young are especially quick to point out the ideological impetus of the Christian tradition that encourages the depletion and waste of the environment. They are also aware that there is a gap between ideals and behavior. This gap is decried by those who would see the churches take a role of leadership in the movement to save the environment.

While it is possible to document the increase in the use of environmental resources, it is impossible to give an adequate list of the scientific and technological advances even in the past ten years. Rather, one particular technological invention can be isolated in order to show its impact on the other major variables that construct our culture. Let us look at the relatively recent invention of what was thought to be a leisure machine—the automobile.

First of all, the automobile has had a profound impact on population. It has made possible the massive movement of people to the suburbs, shifted the geographic sites of principal manufacturers, displaced agricultural workers from rural to urban areas, made the movement of business and industry to the suburbs possible, and increased the geographic mobility of the population. Second, the automobile has created many subsidiary organizations and bureaucracies, such as the tourist industry, the insurance industry, the automotive-service industry, the expanded labor unions, and the highway lobby. In addition, the automobile industry has been the model for the decentralized multidivisional structure of other industrial corporations and has pioneered modern management techniques for these industries. Third, the auto has had an impact on the environment as a consequence of the pollutants that automobiles emit. However, its impact on the environment is more extensive than air pollution. It has also created water pollution (oil in streams from road run-off), noise pollution, land erosion, junkyards, billboards, and roadside litter. Finally, the automobile has changed the values of our society. It has changed patterns of courtship, training and educating children, work habits, leisure time, and family patterns. It has become an identity machine, expanded personal freedom, insulated people from both environmental and human contact, and induced the development of groups of people identified by the type of automobile that they own.

Technological change has affected the churches in ways too numerous to describe. The automobile alone has clearly had an impact on religion. The auto can bring people separated by great distances together to worship in one church. Conversely, the auto can take people from their immediate neighborhood to another much further away in order to attend a particular church service. In effect, increased mobility has given the individual a wider selection of churches from which he may choose.

In addition, there are two other variables, which are more recent and more distinctly American, that have aided in the creation of a new culture. These are (1) the development of a truly mass media and (2) the democratization of the military.

The communications media—books, newspapers, movies, radio, and advertising—have had a dramatic impact on American culture. However, it was the development of television that was the largest component of societal change. By the time he finishes high school, an American child has spent fifteen thousand hours in the classroom, but eighteen thousand hours in front of a TV set. In 1967, fifty-five million families spent seven to eight hours a day with the television set turned on. Yet just twenty years before there were only seventy-five thousand TV sets in the entire country.

The impact of this instrument of leisure has not really been assessed. However, it is known that TV reflects a people simultaneously sentimental, violent, and nostalgic. It is also known that TV has a tendency to relativize our culture, making that which is on TV more likely to be considered both true and real and exposing Americans to groups of people who are unlike themselves. In short, TV has provided most Americans with their first opportunity to see the diversity of opinion and style that is America.

The impact of the mass media on religion, therefore, is to widen our scope of knowledge and our views about different systems of belief. Instantaneous communication has, in effect, been the agent by which religious diversity has been spread.

The final ingredient of the new culture is the democratization of the military. It tends to be forgotten that up until the turn of this century the military was the possession and pastime of the elite. Since World War I, however, the military has become part of all American lives, not only because of the number of men who serve in it but also because it has become pervasive in society. In the United States in 1968, for example, the military had contracts with 2,200 primary contractors and another 100,000 subcontractors. Its monies flowed into 363 of the nations 435 congressional districts, and some 5,300 cities and towns had at least one defense plant or company. Since the turn of the century the United States has, in fact, become a militarized culture.

Since the military has infiltrated the lives of most Americans in some way, it has had a direct impact on religious institutions in that it has brought individuals representing nearly all American religions under its influence. More important, it has inculcated a set of values that are inconsistent with many of the ideals of the Judeo-Christian tradition.

Changes in the cultural context (population, organization, environmental resources, science-technology, mass media, and the military) have indeed produced a new culture. This culture is vastly different from that which existed at the time of the first Reformation, when most mainline churches were established, and is not one in which the institutional churches are either ideologically or organizationally at home.

In creating a new culture that challenges the traditional churches, the changes in the cultural context have also encouraged tensions in another important system of religious beliefs. In particular, the militarization of American culture and the questions of meaning that it has engendered have hastened, if not precipitated, the demise of certain cherished beliefs.

The Breakdown of Civil Religion

The cultural context has not only relativized the importance of traditional expressions of religion but also fractured America's common religion and opened the religious marketplace to different expressions and forms.

Robert Bellah has argued that alongside denominational religion in the United States,[10] there exists an elaborate and well-institutionalized civil religion. He further argues that the common and public element of religious orientation that Americans share is their civil religion. It was crucial in the development of American institutions and still provides a religious dimension for the whole fabric of American life, including the political sphere.

Bellah finds evidence for civil religion in the words and ideas of our founding fathers. Washington, Jefferson, and Franklin refer in their public pronouncements to a God who is not specifically Christian and who is more related to law, order, and right than to love and salvation. Yet the God of civil religion has a special purpose—to establish a new social order that should be an example to other nations.

The civil religion, born in the Revolutionary War, gained impetus after the Civil War. The Civil War introduced the themes of death, sacrifice, and rebirth into the civil religion. These themes found their embodiment in the person of Abraham Lincoln, the man who was sacrificed so that the nation might live with renewed integrity. The writings of Lincoln were revered as the new testament of American civil religion.

10. Robert N. Bellah, "Civil Religion in America," in *Daedalus*, 96, no. 1 (1967), 1–21.

After the Civil War, civil religion found ritualistic expression in the establishment of national cemeteries for "those who gave their lives, that the nation might live," the establishing of Thanksgiving Day as a national holiday in order to integrate the family into the national cult, and the establishment of Memorial Day to do the same for the local community. The public school system served as the vehicle for teaching and expressing the civil religion. Finally, a recent and articulate expression of the civil religion appeared in the inaugural address of the first Catholic president. On the occasion of his inauguration, President Kennedy, who was to be martyred for the national faith, both recognized the impact of the cultural complex and reaffirmed the civil religion.

> The world is very different now. For man holds in his mortal hands the power to abolish all forms of human poverty and to abolish all forms of human life. And yet the same revolutionary beliefs for which our forebears fought are still at issue around the globe—the belief that the rights of man come not from the generosity of the state but from the hand of God. . . . Finally, whether you are citizens of America or of the world, ask of us the same high standards of strength and sacrifice that we shall ask of you. With a good conscience our only sure reward, with history the final judge of our deeds, let us go forth to lead the land we love, asking His blessing and His help, but knowing that here on earth God's work must truly be our own.[11]

These words were spoken in 1961. Since that time the curious nexus between politics and religion in the United States has been broken. The civil religion, fashioned out of the events of the Revolutionary and Civil Wars, was shattered in the crisis of national meaning unleashed by the Vietnam War. It is now less possible to seek transcendence through the State.

This is not to say that civil religion does not have a sizeable number of believers; it surely does. However, it is no longer a consensual religion. Just as the Civil War constituted a threat to the nation and its civil religion, the Vietnam War has produced a large number of unbelievers.

Perhaps the crisis in civil religion is most dramatically exemplified by the controversy surrounding the Berrigan brothers. Denominational religion has traditionally supported the civil religion. Yet the Berrigans are two visible representatives of denominational religion who are not believers in the civil religion. As a result, they have been subject to

11. *Ibid.*, pp. 1–2.

severe criticism from within denominational religion as well as to civil action by the State.

Finally, the largest percentage of disbelievers is in that cohort of young people who are asked to serve it. Correspondingly, the believers tend to be in the age group of Americans who have served the civil religion. Belief in national transcendence is one of those issues that divide generations in the country. To understand better those who do not believe in this mode of transcendence and the options that they have developed, it is first necessary to assay the dimensions of the youth culture.

The Youth Culture

The result of the variables in the cultural complex was not only the production of a new culture, a technoculture, but also the production of a counter-culture. This is a culture in opposition to the values of the dominant culture and is populated mostly by that large segment of the population under twenty-five years of age.

The cultural complex generated a mass society whose primary values were bureaucratic, scientific, and impersonal. In contrast, the parents in this society treated their children more humanistically than any other generation of young people had been treated. Technocratic society provided them the opportunity of being the best fed, healthiest, best educated, and wealthiest generation of young people the world has yet produced. It treated them humanistically and personally; yet it did not prepare them for the transition to the impersonalism and collectivism of the adult world. The result was that young people turned against the culture of their elders. Since they constituted such a large percentage of the population, they began a bargaining process with the larger culture that has been moderately successful. They have pitted their humanistic value structure against the values of the technoculture.

What are the values of the youth counter-culture? A quick reading of Theodore Roszak's *The Making of the Counter Culture* and Charles Reich's *The Greening of America* reveals that their values are the obverse of those produced by the cultural complex.[12] The current generation of middle-class WASP youth is first of all antitechnological and deeply personalistic. They are opposed to the Vietnam War, tend to reject the corporate state, are open to any and all experience, tend to reject the competitive doctrine of life, are skeptical about analytical

12. Theodore Roszak, *The Making of the Counter Culture* (New York: Doubleday and Company, Inc., 1969); Charles Reich, *The Greening of America* (New York: Random House, Inc., 1970). See also: Philip Slater, *In Pursuit of Loneliness: American Culture at the Breaking Point* (Boston: The Beacon Press, 1970).

thought, are antibureaucratic, see pop and rock groups as the real prophets of their generation, and show an unprecedented penchant for mystery, magic, and miracle, as exemplified by their interest in drugs, the occult, and the Jesus movement.

In addition to rejecting the technoculture, the youth culture has rejected the religions of the larger culture—including its civil religion. They see no such totalistic world views and no compelling unifying symbols. Instead, they have created a new religious style whose goal is personal transcendence but which does not necessarily depend on any superempirical deity.

The religions of the counter-culture have arisen in response to the legitimacy of subcults that the cultural context has provided, the breakdown of a totalistic civil religion in America, the increasing latitude with which the churches view new forms of religious expression, and the development of a unique youth counter-culture.

RELIGION IN THE
AGE OF AQUARIUS

The first section of this book is entitled, "Religion in the Age of Aquarius." The entire section is devoted to an interview between Professor Harvey Cox and T George Harris, the editor of *Psychology Today*. Harvey Cox is the theologian-sociologist whose two most famous books, *The Secular City* and *Feast of Fools*, both recorded and helped to create the religious trends of the Age of Aquarius. The interview took place in the spring of 1970 in California at the height of the Aquarian Age. It was at a time of transition. The drug scene was shifting to the widespread use and approval of marijuana and away from LSD, which was being attacked as psychologically and physiologically harmful; occultism was beginning to move away from its association with odd and infirm old people who were interested in flying saucers and astral projection to the youth culture; and the Jesus movement, although it existed, had not yet received widespread media attention.

Nevertheless, Professor Cox accurately discerns the moods in the Age of Aquarius that were to crystalize and become the movements of the post-Aquarian age. He uses evidence that ranges from the writings of Herbert Marcuse, Norman O. Brown, Michael Polanyi, and Teilhard de Chardin to the music of John Cage and the theatre of Antonin Artaud to indicate that the religious mood of the Aquarian Age was one of interest in transcendence, festivity, ecstasy, ritual, fantasy, and celebration.

Cox concludes his conversation by noting that "some form will rise out of the present resurgence of spiritual concern." The remainder of this book explores the forms that a renewed spiritual concern has assumed in the post-Aquarian age.

RELIGION IN THE AGE OF AQUARIUS: A CONVERSATION WITH HARVEY COX & T GEORGE HARRIS

T GEORGE HARRIS: Do you worry, as a theologian, about the general resurgence of superstition and magic? What do you do when students ask about your zodiac sign?

HARVEY COX: You know, I hate to admit it, but they did bug me at first. When somebody would come up and say, "What's your sign?" I used to say, "I don't know. I'm not interested in that stuff." Then I got to the point where I would say in my skeptical Harvard-professor voice, "If you believe there is really some correlation between signs and character, you ought to tell me what sign I am. What sign am I?" Mine was the typical rationalistic approach: "Look at me. Ask me questions. Guess. Let's test it."

Sometimes they would play my game, but it was wrong. I now know why. Do you know what people are saying when they ask your sign? They are saying *I want to relate to you, to be intimate with you in this kooky, interesting, groovy way—a way that is going to blow the minds of those goddamned rationalists. The logical people who have organized our society have defined us into categories that we can't live in.*

Well, that's true. There's no room to move around in, to grow in, in these little boxes reserved for white people, Protestants, Jews, men, women, students, Americans, Russians, Democrats, suburbanites, New Left, rich people, poor. The whole thing is sick, and we can't do without some kind of empathy.

So along comes this absolutely weird group of categories unrelated to social status or anything else. Nobody's defining you, and you're not putting a tag on him. If you're a Taurus and I'm a Taurus, my god, immediately we've got a secret intimacy. We enter into this little conspiracy . . .

HARRIS: . . . like prisoners talking a secret slang . . .

COX: . . . yeah, you and I have this little conspiracy going against the prisonkeepers, the people who put down everything that is not scientifically demonstrable or socially presentable. So we find our own way to define ourselves.

HARRIS: I'm always afraid my sign, Libra, will be a turnoff.

COX: Don't worry, the possibilities are unlimited. See, there are earth signs, air signs, water signs and fire signs. The air sign goes with the earth sign, and the water sign goes with the fire sign, or something like that. And there are other relationships connecting them up. If this doesn't pan out, there's the really esoteric thing about moon signs. You could be a Capricorn born under an Aries moon. It's such an intricate and general-purpose set of symbols that you can use it to build whatever relationship you want.

The astrology trip is a form of play, of relating to each other in ways we don't have to take too seriously until we know we want to. In a broader sense, astrology and drugs and Zen are forms of play, of testing new perceptions of reality without being committed to their validity in advance—or ever.

HARRIS: That word *play* keeps cropping up. In the new book, *The Feast Of Fools*, you develop a general theory of play to make a radical indictment of the work-compulsive society.

COX: I'm not alone, of course, in feeling that in our frantic rush to affluence we have paid a high price in psychic damage. The convincing evidence is beginning to come out of psychology and anthropology. It suggests that we have almost lost, or mutilated, our gift for true festivity and celebration, for pure imagination and playful fantasy.

Two French psychologists, Roger Frétigny and André Virel, began some time ago to use what they call "directed fantasy" in therapy. What I like about their work is that they related their findings to previous studies of mental imagery in anthropology and comparative religion. I think it has immeasurable importance to theology—and not just to theology. It isn't just the church but all of Western culture that has in the name of efficiency become the tribe that lost its head.

Frétigny and Virel talk about four states of consciousness—imaginative, active, reflexive and contemplative. Each has a significant function. The imaginative, of which fantasy is the best example, not only systematizes the materials of experience; it also takes apart both materials and systems in order to construct new configurations. They show how merely rational thought leaves the mind "incurably crippled in a closed and ossified system." It can only extrapolate from the past.

Persons and groups establish rhythms of movement back and forth between the world of facts and the world of fantasies. In tribal societies the period of group fantasy corresponds to the seasonal celebrations of the myths and legends of the tribe. In more complex societies the period is not as well marked and may come less frequently. Virel and Frétigny speculate that a culture such as ours may devote obsessive attention to the fact world for centuries, then move into an era of imaginative creativity and heightened fantasy.

HARRIS: Are we headed that way now?

COX: Maybe, though today's partial rebirth of fantasy may be a deceptive flush on the cheek of a dying age. We're overdue. We have spent the last few hundred years with our cultural attention focused dourly on the "outside" factual world—exploring, investigating and mastering it.

Those who had a penchant for fantasy never really felt at home. They were even driven out of religious institutions, the shelter where the fantasies of the mystic would normally be cherished and cultivated. Christianity, especially its Protestant versions, conned itself, and got conned, into providing the spiritual cement and stick-and-carrot values for Western industrialization. Only in the black church and in folk Catholicism such as Mexico has do you find much of Christ's festive spirit still alive.

HARRIS: And the Methodists have cut the gut-busting tunes out of the *Cokesbury Hymnal*. You have to go to a bar to sing an ecstatic hymn.

Cox: Sure. A bar certainly is one of the few places remaining where you can really let go without somebody taking you seriously. You can play.

It's my conviction that conventional religion has declined not because of the advance of science or the spread of education or any of the reasons normally advanced for secularization. The reason is simple but hard to see because it is embedded in our total environment: the tight, bureaucratic and instrumental society—the only model we've known since the industrial revolution—renders us incapable of experiencing the nonrational dimensions of existence. The absurd, the inspiring, the uncanny, the awesome, the terrifying, the ecstatic—none of these fits into a production- and efficiency-oriented society. They waste time, aren't dependable. When they appear we try to ban them by force or some brand-name therapy. Having systematically stunted the Dionysian side of the whole human, we assume that man is naturally just a reliable, plane-catching Apollonian.

The blame for this distortion usually gets hung on something called "puritanism" or the "Protestant ethic." But that analysis, I believe, is not entirely adequate. No religion yet tested seems to stand unbent by the pressure of the managerial faith known as "Economic Development." Communism, nationalism and other ideologies have gone the same route elsewhere on the globe.

Harris: So how does anybody see out, let alone break out?

Cox: We are never completely the captives of our culture or its language. People all over the world are turning, often desperately, to the overlooked corners and freaks that were never completely systematized. Hence our fascination for pop art—and gloriously, for Fellini's films—with the junk and rejects of the industrial process. Also with the slippery stuff that never found a place in it: astrology, madness, witches, drugs, non-Western religions, palmistry and mysticism, shoddy or serious.

Even the current preoccupation with sex and violence can, to some extent, be understood in terms of this reaction. Both blood and sperm are explosive, irregular, feeling-pitched, messy and inexplicably fascinating. You can't store either one safely in the humming memory of an IBM 360, to be smoothly printed out only when needed in the program. To use a theological term, they *transcend* routine experience.

HARRIS: In *The Secular City*, which stirred up many sociologists and city planners, you argued that urban-age man has become the creator of his own world, heaven or hell, including his value system. We can't blame it on fate or God anymore. With that weight on our heads, you now urge us, in *Feast*, to go dancing in the streets.

COX: Maybe I've learned something. Must there be a gap between those who are working and hoping for a better world and those for whom life is affirmative, a celebration? Must the radicals and revolutionaries—the *new militants*—be at cross purposes with the *neo-mystics*—the hippies and Yippies and all those who are experimenting with new styles of being? I think not, and I hope not. They are, I think, tied together.

So *Feast* is not a recantation of *Secular City*; it's an extension, a recognition that the changes we need are much more fundamental than I thought five years ago, and that the method for achieving them must be much more drastic. Man actually took charge of his own history back in the 19th Century. In *City* I was trying to help us face that fact—defatalization—on the conscious level and work out the consequences. In *Feast* the point is that we can't handle the burden of making history if we are ourselves buried in it, unaware of the timeless dimension that we touch only in fantasy and festivity.

Have you noticed, George, how the past has become an intolerable weight? Except for conservatives who want to use the good-old-days as a club to beat everybody else with, people have a desperate impulse to destroy the past, to curse it, blow it up, burn it. That impulse explains the popularity of books like Norman O. Brown's *Life Against Death* and *Love's Body*. Brown calls on us to "be ready to live instead of making history, to enjoy instead of paying back old scores and debts, and to enter that state of Being which has the goal of Becoming." He begins with Freud's view that repression is the price we pay for civilization, and he thinks the price is exorbitant. History to Brown is not just one damned thing after another; it's one big mistake. He wants to get away from it all.

More calmly, Claude Lévi-Strauss and other French structuralists suggest that we are all over-committed to decision-making, temporal aims and historical objectives. Lévi-Strauss argues that Jean-Paul Sartre, the philosopher of free decision and human world-making, must be left behind.

Much of music and theater seeks to immolate the past quite literally. Take John Cage, for instance. He's certainly the most self-conscious avant-gardist in American music. He undermines the whole axiom of continuity by eliminating the idea of melody. He wants us to listen to one sound at a time, not to hear it in terms of the note that came before it.

In his theater of cruelty, Antonin Artaud invited playwrights to deal in the raw, instant aspects of existence. Lights should be selected not to enhance the play but to blister the eyes of the audience. He wanted to destroy our veneration of what had been done so that we would have to create life in our own idiom. Since Artaud, theater has been used to shock, outrage and seduce the audience out of cool spectator seats to participate in violence, magic and, at times, in joy.

HARRIS: Are you putting down such things as guerrilla theater?

COX: Hell, no. Artaud's mix of spoken and written work lights up the visionary quality of some of the student radicals, the ones who are insistently anti-ideological. Cage, on the other hand, symbolizes the mystical, Dionysiac, experience-believing portion of the present generation: the *now* mentality that is dedicated to pursuit of direct experience—erotic, visual or auditory.

There's a close connection between sensory overload and sensory deprivation. John Lilly discovered in his experiments that for a man suspended in dark silence, a tiny stimulus becomes agonizingly intense. Now go the other way. With an acid-rock band imploding you with sound and a light show chopping your eyeballs, you are totally isolated and must turn intensely inward. It's not exactly like silent contemplation, but its one way to cut yourself off from this harried culture.

Why bother? Is there any reason for people's desperate impulse to cut out of the orderly, tense roles assigned to us? Despite the battles between Christianity and Marxism, both have tended to harness us into a sense of doing whatever history bids us do. "History" is the name we give the horizon of consciousness within which we live. It's all we see. We've lost sight of the larger environment—the cosmic phenomena open to us through intuition, awe and ecstasy—because of our enormous self-consciousness about the events of the past, present and future. Michael Polanyi calls this larger reality the "tacit dimension." Teilhard de Chardin called it the "divine milieu." History is defined by time; the cosmic circle suggests eternity. To be fully human we need to be in touch with both—to apprehend, as T. S. Eliot said, the point of intersection of the timeless with time.

Gestalt psychologists and Marshall McLuhan have both pointed out the necessity for an "anti-environment," the background needed to frame anything before we can see it. If something fills our whole environment, we can't see it.

HARRIS: The fish, Marshall says, did not discover water.

Cox: Or the Age of Aquarius. Anyway, without a timeless perspective, a frame, we cannot regain the humility, the humor to see ourselves and our time honestly or the courage to act sensibly upon our insights. Otherwise we are driven to desperate attempts to "solve" everything. Richard L. Rubenstein wrote in *After Auschwitz* that the West's logical impulse toward solutions could but lead to the Nazi ovens, the "final solution."

HARRIS: Does theology have a way out?

Cox: It will, but not without a little help from its friends—the artists, the students and the social scientists. Most of the sophisticated, critical theology being written today—and this has been true for several decades—comes out of the 19th Century discovery of the historically conditioned character of our tradition, of our Bible, of our encyclicals and rituals. Everything in conventional religion has become second-hand. We are allowed to feel it *only* through careful study of the people who first experienced it long, long ago.

Look, my thesis here is that the sociology of religion is posing problems that theology has to give attention to now—the problems of present experience. Theology has to go much deeper into the social sciences, which suffer from an overweening presentism but can offset the obsessional past in theology. Ever since Emile Durkheim, sociologists have been laying the base for systematic study of the nonhistoric dimension of experience, often without meaning to. I tried to open up this prospect in *Feast*, but to go further I need to do a technical book on theology and the social sciences.

HARRIS: Marcello Truzzi . . . has done a paper on contemporary witchcraft and Satanism, Harvey. He's positive that the upsurge is trivial because the people involved are not serious about it.

COX: That's exactly the reason it's important—people are playing with new perceptions. It's not just the girls who join witches' covens or put on benign hexes. Arthur Waskow reports in *Liberation* on the whole range of rituals among radical groups, who at times are too serious to play in the way that I mean it. They have underground churches, exorcism, Buddhist communities, immolations, confessionals, tie-dye vestments, burn-the-money offerings, encounter groups, monastic contemplations, Indian runes, freedom Seders, commune liturgies, the whole bit. Did you ever notice how often Herbert Marcuse, whose writings gave the New Left its early base, uses the word "transcendent"? A friend of mine went through Marcuse's *One Dimensional Man* underscoring each use of the word. He had marks on just about every page.

HARRIS: Irving Kristol makes a good case in *Fortune* for Marcuse's being more of a religious figure than an intellectual leader.

COX: In many ways that's true, though I'm sure Kristol means it to be a putdown.

The search for new perceptions, however, isn't limited to radicals or neo-mystics. I noticed a while back that my students were reading—really hooked on—six books that ordinarily would not seem to have anything in common. Here they are:

Stranger in a Strange Land, Robert Heinlein's science fiction on the human-from-Mars. Valentine Michael Smith, the hero, could "grok," that beautiful verb for total comprehension, in a way that we earthlings have trained ourselves not to do.

I Ching, the "book of changes" or the sacred books of ancient China.

The Double Helix, the account of how the genetic code was broken—by imagining pretty molecular structures and finding out which one could, by inference, be assumed to exist. Also, there were so many completely nonscientific factors—trying to beat Linus Pauling, and coping with ill-tempered Rosie, the chick in the next lab.

The Teachings of Don Juan, Carlos Castaneda's account of the romantic who refused to see things as practical men did, and do.

The Politics of Experience, psychiatrist R. D. Laing's wild, wonderful application of the theory that schizophrenia is double vision, a survival reaction.

The Mind of the Dolphin, John C. Lilly's research on what the comics of the sea say to each other.

These books all deal with unorthodox, often spooky ways of knowing and feeling, even with seeing things as the dolphin does.

But getting into a nonliteral mode of thought, let alone trying to write about it, is nearly impossible for many people. Remember the weekend we had a few years ago, George, at the American Academy of Arts and Sciences? Henry Murray and Talcott Parsons and Martin Marty and David Riesman—a combination of social scientists and theologians—were all sitting around the table. Remember how miffed Daniel Callahan got over the point you made about the emotional content in religion? He called you a Baptist. Well, my Baptist upbringing helps me to respect the experiential, the validity of the Dionysian. You know, Timothy Leary's wife—second wife—was once a Southern Baptist. I remember spending an evening with them on a hillside, lying under the stars up in New York State. She laughed and said to me, "We Baptists are just natural heads." Beautiful. What she meant was, you know, how could a Unitarian ever see a white flash? What liberal Congregationalist ever had a bad trip in church?

HARRIS: Getting back to behavioral studies, what did you mean about Durkheim's opening up the study of religion?

Cox: Oh, he took on very early the sociologists who wanted to get rid of religion. Religion is not a carry-over from the age of superstition, he pointed out, because religious symbols are essential. They unify the social group. Maybe the best behavioral definition of religion is simply that it's the highest order of symbol system—the one by which other symbol systems and metaphors are myths and values of a culture are ultimately legitimatized. The clammy inanities of present church liturgy have no power to bring us together.

HARRIS: And since the religious symbols come out of man's encounter with the suprarational, we've cut ourselves off from the source of unifying values.

Cox: Yes, but to comprehend religion's place in industrial, urban society, you have to look at more than the church. In *The Invisible Religion,* Thomas Luckmann showed that the church has lost its monopoly on religious symbols. Luckmann, who is a German, is very important to me because he showed that we have been looking at far too narrow a phenomenon—the church.

Another guy who has influenced me is Robert Bellah, who teaches sociology at the University of California. Remember Bellah? He did that brilliant paper for *Daedalus* on "civil religions." Focusing on Presidential inaugurals, he caught the religious overtones and rituals in national life.

Wouldn't it be interesting to analyze The Movement as a kind of counter-civil religion emerging in America with, already, its own sacred texts: "I Have a Dream," for instance, and "Damn Americans who Build Coffins," and a section of "Marcuse" and one on "draft-card immolations." Every radical has to find symbols that are extrinsic, esoteric and have the power to keep him from being encapsulated in the existing culture.

Lloyd Warner would have done it right. He's emeritus and not completely acceptable among sociologists today. But Warner used a good methodology for the study of festivity and symbolism. First he went to Central Australia among the Murngin aborigines. One of his focal points is their annual festival, the Kunapipi. You know how Warner worked, everything in excruciating detail, including the different positions of intercourse—the ritual intercourse as opposed to the ordinary kind. Then Warner came back for his Yankee City series. In the fifth of the series, *The Symbolic Life of Americans*, he reported how Yankee City celebrated its 250th Anniversary, just as he had reported the Kunapipi. He concentrated not on where symbols came from—their history—but on how they were appropriated into meaningful ritual, which is the theological problem today.

HARRIS: Sister Mary Corita—I guess she'd rather be known as artist Corita Kent—is appropriating secular symbols like bread wrappers for sacramental meaning.

COX: Corita's enormously important. People saw her as just a cute nun, but she's the chick who saw slogans like "the Pepsi generation" and "come alive" and "care enough to send the best" and all that stuff in a way that would let us appropriate it. With her paintings she lets us say that man's creations, even the venial ones, are sacred.

HARRIS: Maybe the whole pop-art movement is a sacramentalizing of the environment. The artist lets us see it in a fresh way so we can laugh at it and celebrate it.

Cox: Yeah, yeah, Corita's humanizing the environment and also reminding us that the world is, as she says, unfinished. There's a new universe to create. She brings off these two master strokes at once, and she's got the love to put an ironic twist on slogans that have been used for manipulation.

You know about the thing Corita and some of us did at that discotheque, The Boston Tea Party? We called it "An Evening with God." Everybody came, hundreds, and I started out by saying, a little lamely, "This isn't a church. . . ." Somebody in the back yelled, "It *is* a church. . . ." The ushers in beads and 20 wonderful girls in miniskirts passed out the wine and the home-baked bread. Dan Berrigan read his poems and Judy Collins sang. Corita had a rock band and strobe lights going, and pretty soon everybody was dancing in the aisles.

It worked well, maybe too well, because people keep coming back to ask when we're going to do it again. What we want is for them to do their own celebrations, not lean on us.

Post-industrial man is rediscovering festivity. In churches all over the country there's been this eruption of multimedia masses, jazz rituals, folk and rock worship services, new art and dance liturgies. You know, there's always a John Wesley around to wonder why the Devil should have all the good things. Judson Memorial in New York and a few other churches have had "revelations," the nude dancers in psychedelic lights at the altar. Some people oppose the guitar and the leotard in church for the same reasons their forebears opposed the use of the pipe organ—it never had been done before, or so they think. Others reject the festive new liturgies as merely the latest example of the Establishment's exploitation of flashy gimmicks to lure the recalcitrant back into the fold. They've got a point. Ecclesiastical imperialism is always a threat.

What matters is that the renaissance of festivity is comprehensive, and at the moment there's far more of it outside the church than inside. That's why Corita and I used a discotheque, not a church.

We're now working on an Easter service—for April 26, the Byzantine Easter, three weeks after the regular one. We'll sing things like *Amazing Grace*; Arlo Guthrie made it an ecumenical hymn. The liturgical dancers in Boston specialize in getting everybody to participate. In the midst of the multimedia rejoicing we'll have small group interactions and meditation. And the Woodstock

Eucharist, home-baked bread and jugs. It'll start at 4 a.m. in The Boston Tea Party. At 6 a.m. the trumpets will blow for the resurrection of Christ—whatever that means to you. It's bring-your-own theology. We didn't think too many would come, but so many alienated Protestant and Jewish kids want to participate that we can't find enough things for them to do.

HARRIS: Your emphasis on sensuality blows a lot of clerical minds.

COX: So what do we do, pretend that God created us as disembodied spirits? This is not a new question. Suspicion of the flesh has plagued Christianity off and on for most of its history. I suspect that we've inherited a perverted form of Christianity, deodorized and afraid of smell. That's one reason I used the title *Feast of Fools*, which comes from a Medieval celebration. It was not exactly prim and proper. Ordinarily pious priests and townsfolk put on bawdy masks, sang outrageous ditties and generally kept the world awake with revelry and satire. They made sport of the most sacred royal and religious practices. Of course, the feast was never popular with the higher-ups, who recognized that pure revelry is always radical. As the church became more and more worried about its authority, with running things on time, the bureaucrats managed to stamp out the feast, leaving only a memory of it in Halloween and New Year's.

Our feasting is now sporadic and obsessive, our fantasies predictable and our satire politically impotent. Our celebrations do not relate us, as they once did, to the parade of cosmic history or to the great stories of man's spiritual quest. If discovering that people have bodies is one of the risks we have to take, that seems to be a small—indeed pleasant—price to pay.

HARRIS: How about the risks you've taken in antidraft demonstrations?

COX: I had to be pushed into that. The first time I heard about a guy burning a draft card I was horrified, shocked. Then about three years ago some students who had burned their cards had to go over to South Boston Courthouse for their trial. They were beaten and pummeled by a mob and the police wouldn't intervene. Next day I joined the march—you know, just demanding the right of police protection. That now seems like a long time ago. We were only about 60 people—resistance kids with beards and peace symbols and a couple of black marchers and clergy—but a mob of 300 or 400 came throwing rocks and fruit at us. One guy waved a sword at us with a freshly killed chicken on the point and the blood running down. He had a sense of symbolism.

When we got to the church—it was Good Friday—one of the resistance kids spoke first. He had a swollen eye from the day before. He said the only thing he was sorry about was that the police had separated us from the mob, kept us from really having an encounter with those people. My first thought was "this is where I leave you people—you're crazy." And my second thought was, "Something's happening here that I don't understand." He really felt warmth and regard for the people who wanted to beat him up. I started out with my speech, but I couldn't say much. It was a turning point for me.

Then came a student who was going to refuse to take the symbolic step forward in the induction center. But he didn't want it to be a dour affair. Since he was doing it to affirm life, refusing to kill, he got his girl friend to make bread and strawberry jam, and all his friends came with him, girls handing out flowers to the military and being festive. Even the people at their desks got caught in the spirit of it.

This kind of thing upsets many adults, not only because they disagree on ideas but because they think the kids are putting them on. They're afraid they're being had. What they don't understand is the whole idea of festivity and celebration.

HARRIS: You felt that way, as I recall, the first time you went to Esalen Institute.

COX: Well, Allen Ginsberg was there talking about his masturbatory experiences and Gary Snyder was doing guru grunts. Old Jim Pike was there, troubled and outrageous as usual. He was discussing his communication with the other side. Candles and incense. I never felt more like a rigid defender of orthodoxy in my life. But they really changed my teaching style. I was pretty proud of my lecture technique, but they said, "sit down and let's rap."

HARRIS: You're betting on the social sciences to deal with angel feathers, Harvey—things like festivity are too gossamer to inspire serious work.

COX: No, I don't think so. Didn't you publish Jerome L. Singer's research into daydreaming? [See Psychology Today, "The Importance of Daydreaming," April 1968.] He and John Antrobus discovered that fantasies are richer among what sociologists call the "marginality" people—richer among immigrant Italians and Jews, richer still among black Americans. Apparently fantasy thrives among the disenfranchised. The symbolism in the black church, which, being marginal, never lost its festivity, should produce very rich possibilities. We may yet see comparative religion turn from its Protestant fixation on the texts of other faiths—surely a distorted and limiting view—to a more promising study of the whole religious ritual of a culture.

HARRIS: Where does that leave the institutional church?

COX: Some form of institutionalized religious expression is going to survive. Man is not only a religious being but a social one as well. He's not going to accept a completely do-it-yourself approach on anything this central to survival. Oh, the denominational type of Christianity headquartered in skyscrapers with branch offices in the suburbs is fated for rapid extinction, and it can't disappear too quickly for me. Yet, some form will rise out of the present resurgence of spiritual concern.

The figure of Christ is ubiquitous. He is now beginning to appear as Christ the Harlequin: the personification of celebration and fantasy in an age that has lost both. It is a truer sense of Christ than the saccharine, bloodless face we see painted so often. He was part Yippie and part revolutionary, and part something else. On His day of earthly triumph, Palm Sunday, He rode to town on a jackass. One of the earliest representations of Jesus in religious art depicts a crucified figure with the head of an ass. A weak, even ridiculous church somehow peculiarly at odds with the ruling assumption of its day can once again appreciate the harlequinesque Christ.

RELIGION & DRUGS: CHEMICALLY INDUCED MYSTICISM

The discovery of the synthetic drug called Lysergic Acid Diethylamide-25 was the quiet beginning of what has been a profound change in American religion.

There is a long and clear history to the relationship between drugs and religion.[1] The secret potion of the ancient Greek ceremonies probably contained a psychedelic drug. The dried heads of peyote cactus, whose main ingredient is mescaline, were used in a religious context by Aztecs at least three hundred years before Christ was born. The trend has continued to the present day in remote mountain communities in Mexico, among Siberian Shamans, in South American Indian tribes, and—closer to home—by over fifty thousand Indians who belong to the Native American Church. Even mystics in the Western tradition, although they did not use psychedelic drugs, did produce the same effect. They altered their body chemistry by such practices as breathing and postural exercises, sleep deprivation, fasting, prolonged meditation, and sensory deprivation in darkened caves and monastic cells. In all cases in which naturally occurring plants were used, they were used either by a religious functionary such as a priest or shaman to induce a revelatory trance or by the entire religious community to facilitate the religious experiences of prophesy, divination, clairvoyance, or direct transcendence.

Yet this new use of LSD-25 as a vehicle for religious and transcendent experience differs in some crucial respects from earlier usages

1. Humphry Osmond, "A Review of the Clinical Effects of Psychotomimetic Agents," in *Annals of the New York Academy of Science*, 66 (1957), 418–34. See also R. E. Schultes, "Botanical Sources of the New World Narcotics," in *Psychedelic Review* (1963), 145–46.

of hallucinogens in religious ceremonies. First, LSD is a synthetic drug—a product of modern technology rather than a natural drug. Second, unlike the natural substances in the modern world the use of LSD has not been channeled through a religious institution but has been made available without any controls to anyone who has wished to experiment with it. Third, due to the mass media, the use and effects of LSD, rather than being restricted within the boundaries of a religious institution, have permeated the fabric of American society. As a result of these important differences LSD use should not be considered directly comparable to the religious use of natural psychedelic substances.

As early as William James the correlation between drugs (in his case, nitrous oxide) and religious transcendence was recognized.[2] In the 1950s Aldous Huxley described his own religious experience in his famous work *The Doors of Perception* and concluded that such a drug as mescaline could be used to produce mystical experience.[3] The mystical experience has long been considered the epitome of religious experience. It has recently been discovered that LSD can produce something equivalent to or better than the ecstasy and mystery of the mystical experience.[4] In the mystical experience, there are certain universal characteristics that are not restricted to any particular religion, denomination, or culture.[5]

Religion has three distinct aspects: (1) religious ideology, which is a set of rationally stated beliefs and dogma, the product of someone's previous experience, (2) the active expression of religious principles in a system of ethics concerned with the social welfare of self and others, and (3) the nonrational component of religion, an intuitive experience of something sacred beyond oneself that gives one's whole life meaning.[6] It is this third aspect of religion that applies to both the mystical and the psychedelic experience. It is this aspect that makes the psychedelic movement a religious movement.

The mystical experience and the psychedelic experience have common elements. The first is the slowing down or transcendence of time. The past and the future become of little importance; rather there is an

2. William James, *The Varieties of Religious Experience* (New York: Longmans, 1935).

3. Aldous Huxley, *The Doors of Perception* (New York: Harper and Row, Publishers, Inc., 1954).

4. Alan Watts, "Psychedelics and Religious Experience," in *California Law Review*, 56, no. 1 (1968), 74–85.

5. Walter Terence Stace, *Mysticism and Philosophy* (Philadelphia: J. P. Lippincott Company, 1960).

6. Walter Houston Clark, "The Psychedelics and Religion," in Bernard Aaronson and Humphry Osmond, eds., *Psychedelics* (Cambridge, Massachusetts: Schenkman Publishing Company, 1971), pp. 182–95.

ecstatic feeling of the "now," which is coterminous with eternity and infinity.

Both the traditional mystic and the psychedelic mystic experience a sense of undifferentiated unity. On the one hand, they might experience unity in the inner world—within the experiencer—so that there is no distinction between the experiencer and that which he experiences. The experience itself becomes the primary datum of consciousness. On the other hand, both the mystic and the LSD user might experience an external unity that underlies all empirical multiplicity. He feels he is a part of the entire universe. At the same time, both experiences generate a sense of polarity. At one level the experience is one of underlying unity; at another level the subject knows that all aspects of the universe and life are definable only in terms of opposites—that the categories of creation are simply labels to isolate points in the same continuum. Next, both experiences are intensely emotional. The mystic writes about the tears of joy, the sense of peace, and the ecstatic afterglow of his experience. So do many LSD users. The mystic might feel that words are inadequate to describe his experience, and so does the LSD user. The mystic knows that his experience is not normal or everyday experience and will not be permanent, and so does the LSD user. The mystic gains an intuitive knowledge of an ultimate reality. This knowledge is authoritative and seems more certain than the experience of ordinary reality. He experiences an authoritative insight into existence in general and into his personal, finite self—and so does the LSD user. The mystic often experiences the feeling that he is the Godhead because God is all there is. Although this mystical experience is often couched in ambiguous terms or terms that will not be offensive to his Christian tradition, it is an experience similar to that of the psychedelic user. Both see that all existence is a single energy and that this energy is their own being.

Finally, both the mystic and the psychedelic have a sense of enhanced experience and a sense of themselves as a biological organism. This sense of self as an organism engenders feelings of awareness of the complexity and beauty of natural phenomena—an awareness of the simple and natural. Yet with this drive toward simplicity goes a paradoxical drive toward the baroque and ritualistic. The last element common to the mystic and the psychedelic is the impression of inner depth. Indeed, insofar as the psychedelic experience is described as one in which depth is expanded and there is movement away from surface manifestations toward the inner depth of the self, it becomes more and more like the mystical experience. However, it should also be mentioned that both experiences often expose the dark side of the self.

The fact that the LSD experience is a sort of mystical experience seems to have been clearly documented in the empirical literature.[7] However, the best experimental evidence of the production of mystical experience through the use of psychedelics is provided by the famous "Good Friday Experiment" conducted by Walter Pahnke.[8] Dr. Pahnke used twenty theological students in his double-blind study of the effects of psilocybin. All of the subjects were tested beforehand to determine their psychological profiles, and all of them were thoroughly prepared for the experience. Half were given the drug and the other half a placebo that produced a mild reaction; all of the students then attended a lengthy Good Friday service. The experimental group reported overwhelming mystical experiences. They reported encounters with an ultimate reality, with God—in other words, they reported a transcendent experience. In contrast, the control group reported few experiences that could match those of the experimental group in either depth or intensity. In addition, Pahnke found in a follow-up study six months later that the lives of many in the experimental group had been transformed. They reported that as a result of their experience they were more intensely involved in the lives of others; they were more sensitive to the needs of others, more tolerant, more open, and more authentic in their personal relationships.

This study indicates not only that a transcendent experience is a product of the use of psychedelics, but also that if the conditions are controlled and the environment supportive of a religious experience, the majority of the subjects will undergo an experience that they consider religious.

However, in order to understand the impact of psychedelics on the revival of religious interests, it is necessary to move beyond both documenting the experiences of theological students in a controlled environment and measuring the percentage of the population who have experimented with drugs. Rather, to understand the impact of psychedelics it is necessary to view them in terms of their Gestalt. One must look at the

7. Alan Watts, *The Joyous Cosmology: Adventures in the Chemistry of Consciousness* (New York: Pantheon Books, Inc., 1962); R. E. L. Masters and Jean Houston, *The Varieties of Psychedelic Experience* (New York: Holt, Rinehart & Winston, Inc., 1966); Frank Barron, "Motivational Patterns in LSD Usage," in Richard C. De Bold and Russell C. Leaf, eds., *LSD, Man & Society* (Middletown, Conn.: Wesleyan University Press, 1967); J. Blofield, "Consciousness, Energy, Bliss," in Ralf Metzner, ed., *The Ecstatic Adventure* (New York: The Macmillan Company, 1968); Z. M. Schacter, "The Conscious Ascent of the Soul," in R. Metzner, ed., *The Ecstatic Adventure* (New York: The Macmillan Company, 1968).

8. Walter Pahnke, "LSD and Religious Experience," in Richard C. De Bold and Russell C. Leaf, eds., *LSD, Man & Society* (Middletown, Conn.: Wesleyan University Press, 1967).

pattern of the alterations that psychedelics have induced throughout mass society.

Ordinary people can have profound religious experiences like those of the LSD users through the use of psychedelic sounds, lights, pictures, and other devices, such as soft drugs.[9] In effect, what has occurred is the "psychedelization" of our culture. Although the drugs themselves are no longer as readily available or as widely used as previously, their emanations have acquired an independent reality. These emanations can now be seen in certain aspects of the hippie life style—in the arts, in rock music, in fashion, in communal living arrangements, in a new value emphasis—emotion instead of reason, honesty instead of hypocrisy, depth instead of superficiality, spontaneity instead of deliberation, concern with the now instead of concern with the future, the inner life instead of material acquisition, the personal instead of the impersonal —and in a heightened sense of both good and evil. Finally, a God was discovered who was both the "ultimate reality" and the *mysterium tremendum*. It is this indirect effect of psychedelics that is of importance in understanding the resurgence of a sense of the mystical.

It is well known that the use of psychedelic drugs for any purpose is viewed as repugnant by both secular and religious institutions in our society. Since drugs of all descriptions have become a major social problem in the United States, it is somewhat understandable that the agencies of social control would not clearly distinguish between psychedelic drugs and narcotics. But why should the use of a synthetic chemical that produces mystical experiences under controlled conditions be repugnant to the institutional church? Why are not drugs encouraged as are organ music, fasting, and meditation? There are a number of intuitive reasons.

The first reason is that the psychedelic experience is usually described semantically in terms that are more germane to the Eastern religions than to Western Christianity. Western Christianity has few words to describe an experience of unity with the Godhead or the universe. Eastern religions, however, have these words because they believe they describe a potential reality. The Western Judeo-Christian tradition's paucity of such words reflects its resistance to the idea that the inmost self of man can achieve identity with the Godhead in this life. That experience was reserved for Jesus Christ. The Judeo-Christian tradition, unlike the Shinto, Buddhist, Hindu, and Muslim, has a monarchical image of the Godhead. He is the supreme architect and technician. To see or claim to experience identity with such a Godhead, therefore, is interpreted as insubordination. This incompatibility

9. *The New York Times,* August 26, 1970, p. 43.

of the Judeo-Christian religion with the drug ethos helps to explain the sudden popularity of Eastern religions in the United States immediately after the spread of mind-expanding drugs.

Second, this same Judeo-Christian tradition has placed great emphasis on the free will of the individual. Especially with the rise of Protestantism in the 16th century the individual Christian was given great autonomy in his dealings with God. He was seen as a being who exercised free will and who was judged ultimately on the merits of his choices. He was self-determining, self-controlled, and rational in his choices of the appropriate means to a desired end. Obviously that image of man is in conflict with the images that drugs conjure up. Someone who is "drugged" is stereotyped as irrational, out of control, and deprived of free will. Nevertheless, it is somewhat ironic that a religious tradition such as Protestantism, which once stressed individual religious experience to such an extent that it devalued the importance of the corporate church as an intermediary to the Godhead, should now resist the direct experience of God because it is drug-induced.

Another explanation of why the organized churches oppose the use of drugs in religion follows from the previous reason. The use of psychedelic drugs could democratize religious experience and thus subvert the authority of the churches as the legitimate vehicle of the religious experience and the channel through which God relates to man and man to God. If anyone who ingests a drug is able to experience the Godhead without the guidance of the churches, the churches' very existences are threatened. The need for an institutional church becomes less pronounced, and the fact that the mainline denominations are overinstitutionalized is highlighted.

The final reason for religious opposition to psychedelics is the one most often heard. It involves both the "easiness" of a drug-facilitated religious experience and the massive quantity of hallucinogenics available. In the first instance many feel that because a psychedelic mystical experience is relatively easily achieved, it is not bona fide. They believe that a mystical experience must be the product of ascetical self-discipline, physical hardship, and an exemplary life. Undoubtedly this feeling stems from the emphasis on diligence and hard work in the Protestant ethic. However, the empirical research seems to indicate that the resentment is unfounded. Even in the drug-facilitated mystical experience, previous preparation is of paramount importance, and hard work seems to be necessary after the experience if its effects are to last. The other reason for resentment is that the mystical experience becomes available to as many individuals as seek it. It is often phrased this way: What would the country do with one hundred thousand young mystics? And what would we do to one hundred thousand mystics? The question of what influence they could have on our culture is indeed an intriguing one.

The first reading in this section is important because it was written by Timothy Leary. It is more important, however, because it provides a compendium of the naturalistic and experimental research that bears on the relationship between psychedelics and religious experience. Dr. Leary defines the religious experience as ". . . the ecstatic, incontrovertibly certain, subjective discovery of answers to four basic spiritual questions: (1) the Ultimate-Power question, (2) the Life question, (3) the Human-Destiny question, and (4) the Ego question." Using this definition of religious experience he assembles evidence that synthesizes three traditionally conflicting systems of belief and inquiry. Leary maintains that the belief systems of religion, science, and psychedelics each attempt to answer the four basic spiritual questions. The difference between them is that science attempts to provide objective data, while religion and drugs provide subjective, but no less certain, answers to questions of power, life, destiny, and ego. Those aspects of the psychedelic experience that subjects report to be religious in nature involve a direct awareness of the processes that scientists measure.

The second reading discusses the religious and philosophical aspects of both LSD and marijuana. It is drawn from a symposium on consciousness-expanding drugs held at New York University in 1967. In this article, which was edited by Raziel Abelson, Allen Ginsberg argues from his own experience that hallucinogenic drugs are useful in seeking a more intense religious experience. In contrast, Michael Wyschogrod argues that such drugs produce only an imitation of the true religious experience. For him, the spirit of God does not come in a chemical or in a bottle. Furthermore, he feels that instant mysticism is an illusion that merely abets the tendency of modern technology to make our entire lives artificial.

The final reading in this section is only indirectly related to the relationship between drugs and religion. Soon after psychedelics induced a sense of the mysterious, many of the young rejected drugs and turned to Eastern mysticism. Jacob Needleman reflects on the new mystics and evaluates their importance to our culture. The article serves the dual purpose of connecting the psychedelic movement to the Eastern mysticism movement and of providing a theoretical link to the occult, since Eastern mysticism can be thought of as shared mystical occultism.

THE RELIGIOUS EXPERIENCE: ITS PRODUCTION & INTERPRETATION

Timothy Leary

THREE YEARS AGO, ON A SUNNY AFTERNOON IN THE GARDEN OF A Cuernavaca villa, I ate seven of the so-called "sacred mushrooms" which had been given to me by a scientist from the University of Mexico. During the next five hours, I was whirled through an experience which could be described in many extravagant metaphors but which was above all and without question the deepest religious experience of my life.

Statements about personal reactions, however passionate, are always relative to the speaker's history and may have little general significance. Next come the questions "Why?" and "So what?"

There are many predisposing factors—intellectual, emotional, spiritual, social—which cause one person to be ready for a dramatic mind-opening experience and which lead another to shrink back from new levels of awareness. The discovery that the human brain possesses an infinity of potentialities and can operate at unexpected space-time dimensions left me feeling exhilarated, awed, and quite convinced that I had awakened from a long ontological sleep.

A profound transcendent experience should leave in its wake a changed man and a changed life. Since my illumination of August, 1960, I have devoted most of my energies to try to understand the

"The Religious Experience: Its Production and Interpretation," by Timothy Leary. From *Psychedelic Review*, 1965, pp. 191–213. Reprinted by permission of the publisher.

Lecture delivered at a meeting of Lutheran psychologists and other interested professionals, sponsored by the Board of Theological Education, Lutheran Church in America, in conjunction with the 71st Annual Convention of the American Psychological Association, Philadelphia, Bellevue Stratford Hotel, August 30, 1963.

revelatory potentialities of the human nervous system and to make these insights available to others.

I have repeated this biochemical and (to me) sacramental ritual over fifty times personally and, almost every time, I have been awed by religious revelations as shattering as the first experience. During this period I have been lucky enough to collaborate in this work with more than 50 scientists and scholars who joined our various research projects. We have arranged transcendent experiences for over one thousand persons from all walks of life, including 69 full-time religious professionals, about half of whom profess the Christian or Jewish faith and about half of whom belong to Eastern religions.

Included in this roster are two college deans, a divinity college president, three university chaplains, an executive of a religious foundation, a prominent religious editor, and several distinguished religious philosophers. In our research files and in certain denominational offices there is building up a large and quite remarkable collection of reports which will be published when the political atmosphere becomes more tolerant. At this point it is conservative to state that over 75 percent of these subjects report intense mystico-religious responses, and considerably more than half claim that they have had the deepest spiritual experience of their life.[1]

The interest generated by this research led to the formation of an informal group of ministers, theologians and religious psychologists who have been meeting once a month (summers excepted) for over two years, with an average of 20 persons in attendance. In addition to arranging for spiritually oriented psychedelic sessions and discussing prepared papers, this group provided the supervisory manpower for the dramatic "Good Friday" study, and was the original planning nucleus of the organization which assumed sponsorship of our research in consciousness-expansion: IF-IF (the International Federation for Internal Freedom). The generating impulse and the original leadership of IFIF came from a seminar in religious experience, and this fact may be related to the alarm which IFIF aroused in some secular and psychiatric circles.

The "Good Friday" Study, which has been sensationalized recently in the press as "The Miracle of Marsh Chapel," deserves

1. Leary, T., Litwin, G. H., and Metzner, R., "Reactions to Psilocybin Administered in a Supportive Environment," in *J. Nervous & Mental Disease*, 137, no. 6 (December 1963), 561–73.

further elaboration not only as an example of a serious, controlled experiment, involving over 30 courageous volunteers, but also as a systematic demonstration of the religious aspects of the psychedelic revelatory experience. This study was the Ph.D-dissertation research of a graduate student in the philosophy of religion at Harvard University, who is, incidentally, both an M.D. and a Bachelor of Divinity. This investigator set out to determine whether the transcendent experience reported during psychedelic sessions was similar to the mystical experience reported by saints and famous religious mystics.

The subjects in this study were 20 divinity students selected from a group of volunteers. The subjects were divided into five groups of four persons, and each group met before the session for orientation and preparation. To each group were assigned two guides with considerable psychedelic experience. The ten guides were professors and advanced graduate students from Boston-area colleges.

The experiment took place in a small, private chapel, beginning about one hour before noon on Good Friday. The Dean of the Chapel, who was to conduct a three-hour devotional service upstairs in the main hall of the church, visited the subjects a few minutes before the start of the service at noon, and gave a brief inspirational talk.

Two of the subjects in each group and one of the two guides were given a moderately stiff dosage (i.e., 30 mg) of psilocybin, the chemical synthesis of the active ingredient in the "sacred mushroom" of Mexico. The remaining two subjects and the second guide received a placebo which produced noticeable somatic side effects, but which was not psychedelic. The study was triple-blind: neither the subjects, guides, nor experimenter knew who received psilocybin.

Because the dissertation describing this study has not yet been published,[2] any detailed discussion of the results would be premature and unfair to the investigator. I can say, however, that the results clearly support the hypothesis that, with adequate preparation and in an environment which is supportive and religiously meaningful, sub-

---

2. Walter N. Pahnke, *Drugs and Mysticism: An Analysis of the Relationship between Psychedelic Drugs and the Mystical Consciousness.* A thesis presented to the Committee on Higher Degrees in History and Philosophy of Religion, in partial fulfillment of the requirements for the degree of Doctor of Philosophy, Harvard University, Cambridge, Mass., June, 1963.

jects report mystical experiences significantly more than placebo controls.

Our studies, naturalistic and experimental, thus demonstrate that if the expectation, preparation, and setting are spiritual, an intense mystical or revelatory experience can be expected in from 40 to 90 percent of subjects ingesting psychedelic drugs. These results *may be* attributed to the bias of our research group, which has taken the "far-out" and rather dangerous position that there are experiential-spiritual as well as secular-behavioral potentialities of the nervous system. While we share and follow the epistemology of scientific psychology (objective records), our basic ontological assumptions are closer to Jung than to Freud, closer to the mystics than to the theologians, closer to Einstein and Bohr than to Newton. In order to check on this idea, let us cast a comparative glance at the work of other research groups in this field who begin from more conventional ontological bases.

Oscar Janiger, a psychiatrist, and William McGlothlin, a psychologist, have reported the reactions of 194 psychedelic subjects. Seventy-three of these took LSD as part of a psychotherapy program, and 121 were volunteers. The religious "set" would not be expected to dominate the expectations of these subjects. The results, which are abstracted from a paper published in *The Psychedelic Review*,[3] are as follows:

Item	*Percent* Janiger-McGlothlin[a] N = 194
Increased interest in morals, ethics . . .	35
Increased interest in other universal concepts (meaning of life)	48
Change in sense of values	48
LSD should be used for:	
becoming aware of oneself	75
getting new meaning to life	58
getting people to understand each other	42
An experience of lasting benefit	58

[a] non-religious setting

3. "The Subjective After-Effects of Psychedelic Experiences: A Summary of Four Recent Questionnaire Studies." *The Psychedelic Review*, Vol. I, No. 1 (June 1963), 18–26.

Two other studies, one by Ditman *et al.*, another by Savage *et al.*, used the same questionnaire, allowing for inter-experiment comparison. Both Ditman and Savage are psychiatrists, but the clinical environment of the latter's study is definitely more religious (subjects are shown religious articles during the session, etc.). Summarizing the religious items of their questionnaires:

Item	*Percent*	
	Ditman[b]	Savage[c]
	N = 74	N = 96
Feel it [LSD] was the greatest thing that ever happened to me	49	85
A religious experience	32	83
A greater awareness of God or a Higher Power or an Ultimate Reality	40	90

[b] supportive environment
[c] supportive environment & some religious stimuli

Here, then, we have five scientific studies by qualified investigators—the four naturalistic studies by Leary *et al.*,[1] Savage *et al.*,[4] Ditman *et al.*,[5] and Janiger-McGlothlin,[6] and the triple-blind study in the Harvard dissertation mentioned earlier—yielding data which indicate that (1) if the setting is supportive but not spiritual, between 40 to 75 percent of psychedelic subjects will report intense and lifechanging religious experiences; and that (2) if the set and setting are supportive and spiritual, then from 40 to 90 percent of the experiences will be revelatory and mystico-religious.

It is hard to see how these results can be disregarded by those who are concerned with spiritual growth and religious development. These data are even more interesting because the experiments took place during an historical era when mysticism, individual religious ecstacy (as opposed to religious behavior), was highly suspect, and

4. Savage, C.; Harman, W. W.; Fadiman, Jr.; and Savage, E.; "A Follow-up Note on the Psychedelic Experience." Paper delivered at a meeting of the American Psychiatric Association, St. Louis, Mo., May 1963.

5. Ditman, K. S., Haymon, M., and Whittlesey, J. R. B., "Nature and Frequency of Claims Following LSD," in *J. Nervous & Mental Disease*, 134 (1962), 346–52.

6. McGlothlin, W. H., *Long-Lasting Effects of LSD on Certain Attitudes in Normals: An Experimental Proposal* (privately printed, The Rand Corporation, Santa Monica, Calif., June 1962), p. 56. Cf. McGlothlin, W. H., Cohen, S., & McGlothlin, M. S., *Short-Term Effects of LSD on Anxiety, Attitudes, and Performance (Ibid., June 1963)*, p. 15.

when the classic, direct, non-verbal means of revelation and consciousness-expansion such as meditation, yoga, fasting, monastic withdrawal and sacramental foods and drugs were surrounded by an aura of fear, clandestine secrecy, active social sanction, and even imprisonment.[7] The 69 professional workers in religious vocations who partook of psychedelic substances (noted earlier) were responsible, respected, thoughtful, and moral individuals who were grimly aware of the controversial nature of the procedure and aware that their reputations and their jobs might be undermined (and, as a matter of fact, have been and are today being threatened for some of them). *Still* the results read: 75% spiritual revelation. It may well be that the most intense religious experience, like the finest metal, requires fire, the heat of external bureaucratic opposition, to produce the keenest edge. When the day comes—as it surely will—that sacramental biochemicals like LSD will be as routinely and tamely used as organ music and incense to assist in the attainment of religious experience, it may well be that the ego-shattering effect of the drug will be diminished. Such may be one aspect of the paradoxical nature of religious experience.

The Religious Experience

You are undoubtedly wondering about the meaning of this phrase which has been used so freely in the preceding paragraphs. May I offer a definition?

The religious experience is the ecstatic, incontrovertibly certain, subjective discovery of answers to four basic spiritual questions. There can be, of course, absolute subjective certainty in regard to secular questions: "Is this the girl I love? Is Fidel Castro a wicked man? Are the Yankees the best baseball team?" But issues which do not involve the four basic questions belong to secular games, and

7. A continuing present-day instance is the case of members of the Native American Church, a duly constituted and recognized religious denomination numbering almost a quarter of a million adherents. A good popular account of their situation is presented in "Peyote," by A. Stump, in *Saga*, 26, no. 3 (June 1963), 46–49, 81–83. Cf. the Supreme Court's decision, *Oliver v. Udall*, 306 F2d 819 (1962). The most recently proposed legislation against peyote is seen in the *Congressional Record* (House) for December 13, 1963. The most recent revision of W. La Barre's famous book, *The Peyote Cult*, was published by the Shoe String Press in 1970. In 1969 a revised, illustrated paperback was published by Schocken. For a good general statement in another area of research, see "The Hallucinogenic Drugs," by Barron, Jarvik, and Bunnel, in *Sci. Amer.*, 210, no. 4 (April 1964), 29–37.

such convictions and faiths, however deeply held, can be distinguished from the religious. Liturgical practices, rituals, dogmas, theological speculations, can be and too often are secular, i.e., completely divorced from the spiritual experience.

What are these four basic spiritual questions? There is the Ultimate-Power question, the Life question, the Human-Destiny question, and the Ego question.

1. *The Ultimate-Power Question:*
   What is the Ultimate Power or Basic Energy which moves the universe, creates life? What is the Cosmic Plan?

2. *The Life Question:*
   What is life, where did it start, where is it going?

3. *The Human-Destiny Question:*
   What is man, whence did he come, and where is he going?

4. *The Ego Question:*
   What am I? What is my place in the plan?

While one may disagree with the wording, I think most thoughtful people—philosophers or not—can agree on something like this list of basic issues. Do not most of the great religious statements—Eastern or monotheistic—speak directly to these four questions?

Now one important fact about these questions is that they are continually being answered and re-answered, not only by all the religions of the world but also by the data of the natural sciences. Read these questions again from the standpoint of the goals of (1) astronomy-physics, (2) biochemistry, (3) genetics, paleontology, and evolutionary theory, (4) neurology.

We are all aware of the unhappy fact that both science and religion are too often diverted towards secular game goals. Various pressures demand that laboratory and church forget these basic questions and instead provide distractions, illusory protection, narcotic comfort. Most of us dread confrontation with the answers to these basic questions, whether these answers come from science or religion. But if "pure" science and religion address themselves to the same basic questions, what is the distinction between the two disciplines? Science is the systematic attempt to record and measure the energy process and the sequence of energy transformations we call life. The goal is to answer the basic questions in terms of objective, observed public data. Religion is the systematic attempt to provide answers *to the same questions* subjectively, in terms of direct, incontrovertible, personal experience.

Science is a social system which evolves roles, rules, rituals, values, language, space-time locations to further the quest for these goals—these answers. Religion is a social system which has evolved its roles, rules, rituals, values, language, space-time locations to further the pursuit of the same goals—the revelatory experience. A science which fails to address itself to these spiritual goals, which accepts other purposes (however popular), becomes secular, poetical, and tends to oppose new data. A religion which fails to provide direct experiential answers to these spiritual questions becomes secular, political, and tends to oppose the individual revelatory confrontation. R. C. Zaehner,[8] whose formalism is not always matched by his tolerance, has remarked that "experience, when divorced from revelation, often leads to absurd and wholly irrational excesses." Like any statement of polarity the opposite is equally true: revelation, when divorced from experience, often leads to absurd and wholly rational excesses. Those of us who have been researching the area of consciousness have been able to collect considerable sociological data about the tendency of the rational mind to spin out its own interpretations. But I shall have more to say about the political situation in a later section of this paper.

At this point I should like to present my main thesis. I am going to advance the hypothesis that *those aspects of the psychedelic experience which subjects report to be ineffable and ecstatically religious involve a direct awareness of the processes which physicists and biochemists and neurologists measure.*

We are treading here on very tricky ground. When we read the reports of LSD subjects, we are doubly limited. First, *they* can only speak in the vocabulary they know, and for the most part they do not possess the lexicon and training of energy scientists. Second, *we researchers* only find what we are prepared to look for, and too often we think in crude psychological-jargon concepts: moods, emotions, value judgments, diagnostic categories.

In recent months we have re-examined our data and have begun to interview subjects from the perspective of this present hypothesis. The results are interesting. To spell them out in brief detail I am going to review some of the current scientific answers to these four basic questions and then compare them with reports from psychedelic subjects.

8. Zaehner, R. C., *At Sundry Times: An Essay in the Comparison of Religions* (London: Faber & Faber, 1958), p. 57.

(1) THE ULTIMATE-POWER QUESTION

A. *The scientific answers* to this question change constantly—Newtonian laws, quantum indeterminacy, atomic structure, nuclear structure. Today the basic energy is located within the nucleus. Inside the atom,

> a transparent sphere of emptiness, thinly populated with electrons, the substance of the atom has shrunk to a core of unbelievable smallness: enlarged 1000 million times, an atom would be about the size of a football, but its nucleus would still be hardly visible—a mere speck of dust at the center. Yet that nucleus radiates a powerful electric field which holds and controls the electrons around it.[9]

Incredible power and complexity operating at speeds and spatial dimensions which our conceptual minds cannot register. Infinitely small, yet pulsating outward through enormous networks of electrical forces—atom, molecule, cell, planet, star: all forms dancing to the nuclear tune.

The *cosmic design* is this network of energy whirling through space-time. More than 15,000 million years ago the oldest known stars began to form. Whirling disks of gas molecules (driven of course by that tiny, spinning, nuclear force)—condensing clouds—further condensations—the tangled web of spinning magnetic fields clustering into stellar forms, and each stellar cluster hooked up in a magnetic dance with its planetary cluster and with every other star in the galaxy and each galaxy whirling in synchronized relationship to the other galaxies.

One thousand million galaxies. From 100 million to 100,000 million stars in a galaxy—that is to say, 100,000 million planetary systems per galaxy and each planetary system slowly wheeling through the stellar cycle that allows for a brief time the possibility of life as we know it.

Five thousand million years ago, a slow-spinning dwarf star we call the sun is the center of a field of swirling planetary material. The planet earth is created. In five thousand million years the sun's

9. Woltereck, H., *What Science Knows About Life* (New York: Association Press, 1963).

supply of hydrogen will be burned up, the planets will be engulfed by a final solar explosion. Then the ashen remnants of our planetary system will spin silently through the dark infinity of space. And then is the dance over? Hardly. Our tiny solar light, which is one of one hundred thousand million suns in our galaxy, will scarcely be missed. And our galaxy is one of a thousand million galaxies spinning out and up at rates which exceed the speed of light—each galaxy eventually burning up, to be replaced by new galaxies to preserve the dance equilibrium.

Here in the always changing data of nuclear physics and astronomy is the current scientific answer to the first basic question—material enough indeed for an awesome cosmology.

B. *Psychedelic reports* often contain phrases which seem to describe similar phenomena, subjectively experienced.

(a) I passed in and out of a state several times where I was so relaxed that I felt open to a total flow, over and around and through my body (more than my body) . . . . All objects were dripping, streaming, with white-hot light or electricity which flowed in the air. It was as though we were watching the world, just having come into being, cool off, its substance and form still molten and barely beginning to harden.

(b) Body being destroyed after it became so heavy as to be unbearable. Mind wandering, ambulating throughout an ecstatically-lit indescribable landscape. How can there be so much light—layers and layers of light, light upon light, all is illumination.

(c) I became more and more conscious of vibrations—of the vibrations in my body, the harp-strings giving forth their individual tones. Gradually I felt myself becoming one with the Cosmic Vibration. . . . In this dimension there were no forms, no deities or personalities—just bliss.

(d) The dominant impression was that of entering into the very marrow of existence . . . . It was as if each of the billion atoms of experience which under normal circumstances are summarized and averaged into crude, indiscriminate wholesale impressions was now being seen and savored for itself. The other clear sense was that of cosmic relativity. Perhaps all experience never gets summarized in any inclusive overview. Perhaps all there is, is this everlasting congeries of an infinite number of discrete points of view, each summarizing the whole from its perspective.

(e) I could see the whole history and evolution along which man has come. I was moving into the future and saw the old cycle of peace and war, good times and bad times, starting to re-peat, and I said, "The same old thing again, oh God! It has changed though, it is different," and I thought of the rise of man from animal to spiritual being. But I was still moving into the future and I saw the whole planet destroyed and all history, evolution, and human efforts being wiped out in this one ultimate destructive act of God.

Subjects speak of participating in and merging with pure (i.e., content-free) energy, white light; of witnessing the breakdown of macroscopic objects into vibratory patterns, visual nets, the collapse of external structure into wave patterns, the awareness that every-thing is a dance of particles, sensing the smallness and fragility of our system, visions of the void, of world-ending explosions, of the cyclical nature of creation and dissolution, etc. Now I need not apol-ogize for the flimsy inadequacy of these words. We just don't have a better experiential vocabulary. If God were to permit you a brief voyage into the Divine Process, let you whirl for a second into the atomic nucleus or spin you out on a light-year trip through the galaxies, how on earth would you describe what you saw, when you got back, breathless, to your office? This metaphor may sound far-fetched and irrelevant, but just ask someone who has taken LSD in a supportive setting.

(2) THE LIFE QUESTION

A. *The scientific answer:* Our planetary system began over five billion years ago and has around five billion years to go. Life as we know it dates back to about one billion years. In other words, the earth spun for about 80 percent of its existence without life. The crust slowly cooled and was eroded by incessant water flow. "Fertile mineral mud was deposited . . . now giving . . . for the first time . . . the possibility of harboring life." Thunderbolts in the mud produce amino acids, the basic building blocks of life. Then begins the ceaseless production of protein molecules, incalcu-lable in number, forever combining into new forms. The variety of proteins "exceeds all the drops of water in all the oceans of the world." Then protoplasm. Cell. Within the cell, incredible beauty and order.

When we consider the teeming activity of a modern city it is difficult to realize that in the cells of our bodies infinitely more complicated processes are at work—ceaseless manufacture, acquisition of food, storage, communication and administration . . . . All this takes place in superb harmony, with the cooperation of all the participants of a living system, regulated down to the smallest detail.[9]

Life is the striving cycle of repetitious, reproductive energy transformations. Moving, twisting, devouring, changing, the unit of life is the cell. And the blueprint is the genetic code, the two nucleic acids—the long, intertwined, duplicating chains of DNA and the controlling regulation of RNA—"which determine the structure of the living substance."

And where is it going? Exactly like the old Hindu myths of cyclical rotation, the astrophysicists tell us that life is a temporary sequence which occurs at a brief midpoint in the planetary cycle. Terrestrial life began around four billion years A.B. ("after the beginning" of our solar cycle) and will run for another two billion years or so. At that time the solar furnace will burn so hot that the minor planets (including Earth) will boil, bubble and burn out. In other planetary systems the time spans are different, but the cycle is probably the same.

There comes an intermediate stage in the temperature history of a planet which can nourish living forms, and then life merges into the final unifying fire. Data here, indeed, for an awesome cosmology.

B. *The psychedelic correlates* of these biological concepts sound like this: confrontation with and participation in cellular flow; visions of microscopic processes; strange, undulating, multi-colored, tissue patterns; being a one-celled organism floating down arterial waterways; being part of the fantastic artistry of internal factories; recoiling with fear at the incessant push, struggle, drive of the biological machinery, clicking, clicking, endlessly, endlessly—at every moment engulfing you. For example:

(a)   My eyes closed, the impressions became more intense. The colors were brilliant blues, purples, and greens with dashes of red and streaks of yellow-orange. There were no easily identifiable objects, only convolutions, prisms, and continuous movement.

(b)   My heart a lizard twitching lithely in my pocket, awaiting the wave again, my flesh sweating as it crawled over my bones, the mountains curved around my heart, the surf crashing against my mucoused lungs, coughing into heart beats, pulsing death to scare me. Futile body. Awaiting the undertow escaping under the wave which crashed so coughingly over my heart, blue lighted into YES. An undertow going UP . . . . The universe has an axis which is not perpendicular, and round it flock the living colors, pulsing eternal involutions.

(c)   I then gradually became aware of movement, a rocking type of movement, like on a roller-coaster, yet I did not move my body at all . . . . With an overwhelming acceleration I was turning around and around, swirling, then shuttling back and forth, like a piece of potassium on water, hissing, sparkling, full of life and fire.

(3) THE HUMAN-DESTINY QUESTION

A. *The scientific answer:* The flame of life which moves every living form, including the cell cluster you call your*self*, began, we are told, as a tiny single-celled spark in the lower pre-Cambrian mud; then passed over in steady transformations to more complex forms. We like to speak of higher forms, but let's not ignore or patronize the single-cell game. It's still quite thriving, thank you. Next, your ancestral fire glowed in seaweed, algae, flagellate, sponge, coral (about one billion years ago); then fish, fern, scorpion, milliped (about 600 million years ago). Every cell in your body traces back (about 450 million years ago) to the same light-life flickering in amphibian (and what a fateful and questionable decision to leave the sea— should we have done it?). Then forms, multiplying in endless diversity—reptile, insect, bird—until, one million years ago, comes the aureole glory of Australopithecus.[10]

The torch of life next passes to the hand-axe culture (around 600,000 years ago) to Pithecanthropus (can you remember watching for the charge of Southern elephants and the sabre-tooth tiger?);

---

10. The fossils of the newly discovered "Homo Habilis" from East Africa are estimated to be 1,750,000 years old. (*N. Y. Times*, March 18, April 3 & 4, 1964. Another estimate traces human origins back about 15 million years!— N. Y. *Times*, April 12, 1964.)

then blazing brightly in the radiance of our great-grandfather Neanderthal man (a mere 70,000 years ago), suddenly flaring up in that cerebral explosion that doubled the cortex of our grandfather Cromagnon man (44,000 to 10,000 years ago), and then radiating into the full flame of recent man, our older Stone Age, Neolithic brothers, our Bronze and Iron Age selves.

What next? The race, far from being culminated, has just begun:

> The development of Pre-hominines Australopithecus . . . to the first emergence of the . . . Cromagnons lasted about . . . fifteen thousand human life-spans . . . . In this relatively short period in world history the hominid type submitted to a positively hurricane change of form; indeed he may be looked upon as one of the animal groups whose potentialities of unfolding with the greatest intensity have been realized. It must, however, by no means be expected that this natural flood of development will dry up with *Homo sapiens recens.* Man will be unable to remain man as we know him now, a modern sapiens type. He will in the courses of the next hundreds of millennia presumably change considerably physiologically and physically.[11]

B. *The psychedelic correlate:* What does all that evolutionary business have to do with you or me or LSD or the religious experience? It might, it just might, have a lot to do with very current events. Many, and I am just bold enough to say most, LSD subjects say they experience early forms of racial or sub-human species evolution during their sessions. Now the easiest interpretation is the psychiatric: "Oh yes, hallucinations. Everyone knows that LSD makes you crazy, and your delusions can take any psychotic form." But wait; not so fast. Is it entirely inconceivable that our cortical cells, or the machinery inside the cellular nucleus, "remembers" back along the unbroken chain of electrical transformations that connects every one of us back to that original thunderbolt in the pre-Cambrian mud? Impossible, you say? Read a genetics text. Read and reflect about the DNA chain of complex protein molecules that took you as a uni-celled organism at the moment of your conception and planned every stage of your natural development. Half of that genetic blueprint was handed to you intact by your mother, and

11. Schenk, G., *The History of Man* (Philadelphia and New York: Chilton Co., 1961), pp. 56–57.

half from your father, and then slammed together in that incredible welding process we call conception.

"You," your ego, your good-old American-social-self, have been trained to remember certain crucial secular game landmarks: your senior prom, your wedding day. But is it not possible that others of your ten million brain cells "remember" other critical survival crossroads like conception, intra-uterine events, birth? Events for which our language has few or no descriptive terms? Every cell in your body is the current-carrier of an energy torch which traces back through millions of generation-transformations. Remember that genetic code?

You must recognize by now the difficulty of my task. I am trying to expand your consciousness, break through your macroscopic, secular set, "turn you on," give you a faint feeling of a psychedelic moment, trying to relate two sets of processes for which we have no words—speed-of-light energy-transformation processes and the transcendent vision.

I'm going to call for help. I could appeal to quotes from Gamow the cosmologist, or Eiseley the anthropologist, or Hoyle the astronomer, or Teilhard de Chardin the theological biologist, or Aldous Huxley the great visionary prophet of our times, or Julian Huxley whose pharmacological predictions sound like science-fiction. I could call upon a hundred articulate scientists who talk in dazed poetry about the spiritual implications of their work. Instead, I am going to read a passage by the German anthropologist Egon Freiherr von Eickstedt. The topic is the spiritual attitude of Australopithecus. The point is that this description of the world-view of a tiny monkeyman who lived a million years ago could be a quote from any one of a hundred LSD reports I've read in the last three years. Von Eickstedt's research leads him to say that,

> In the way of experience there is dominant, throughout, a kaleidoscopic interrelated world. Feeling and perception are hardly separated in the world of visions; space and time are just floating environmental qualities. . . . Thus the border between I and not-I is only at the border of one's own and actually experienced, perceptible world. . . . But this by no means denotes merely bestial brutality and coarseness which is so erroneously and often ascribed to the beginnings of humanity. Quite the reverse. The thymality within his own circle means just the opposite, tenderness, goodness and cheerfulness, and allows with complete justification the pre-

sumption of a picture of intimate family life and the specific teaching of the children, also need of ornament, dance and much
happiness. Thus the extremes of feeling swing with the mood
between fear and love, and the dread of the unknowable. . . .[12]

We have in our files an LSD report from a world-renowned
theologian with astonishing parallels to this quotation.

The best way I can describe the experience as a whole is to
liken it to an emotional-reflective-visual kaleidoscope . . . . Experiences involving these three components kept dissolving continuously from one pattern into another. Emotionally the patterns
ranged from serene contentment and mild euphoria to apprehen-
sion which bordered on, but never quite slipped into, alarm. But
overwhelmingly they involved (a) astonishment at the absolutely
incredible immensity, complexity, intensity and extravagance of
being, existence, the cosmos, call it what you will. Ontological
shock, I suppose. (b) The most acute sense of the poignancy,
fragility, preciousness, and significance of all life and history. The
latter was accompanied by a powerful sense of the responsibility of
all for all . . . . Intense affection for my family . . . . Importance
and rightness of behaving decently and responsibly.

(4) THE EGO QUESTION

A. *The scientific answer:* The question "Who am I?" can be answered at many levels. Psychologists can describe and explain your
psychogenesis and personal evolution. Sociologists and anthropologists can explain the structure of the tribal games which govern
your development. Biologists can describe your unique physical
structure. But the essence of you and "you-ness" is your consciousness. You are not a psychological or social or bodily robot. No external description comes close. What cannot be measured, replaced,
understood by any objective method is your consciousness. And
where is this located? In your nervous system. The secular-game
engineers can entertain you with their analyses of your macroscopic
characteristics, but the biochemical neurologist is the man to listen
to. He is the person who can locate "you" in the five-billion-year
sequence by describing the capacities of your cortex. Your consciousness is a biochemical electrical process.

The human brain, we are told,

12. *Ibid.,* p. 238.

is composed of about 10 billion nerve cells, any one of which may connect with as many as 25,000 other nerve cells. The number of interconnections which this adds up to would stagger even an astronomer—and astronomers are used to dealing with astronomical numbers. The number is far greater than all the atoms in the universe . . . . This is why physiologists remain unimpressed with computers. A computer sophisticated enough to handle this number of interconnections would have to be big enough to cover the earth.[13]

Into this matrix floods "about 100 million sensations a second from . . . [the] various senses." And somewhere in that ten-billion-cell galaxy is a tiny solar system of connected neurons which is aware of your social self. Your "ego" is to your cortex what the planet Earth is to our galaxy with its 100,000 million suns.

B. *The psychedelic answer* to the "I" question is the crux of the LSD experience. Most of the affect swirls around this issue. As Erik Erikson reminds us, it's hard enough to settle on a simple tribal role definition of "Who am I?" Imagine the dilemma of the LSD subject whose cortex is suddenly turned on to a much higher voltage, who suddenly discovers his brain spinning at the speed of light, flooded by those 100 million sensations a second. Most of the awe and reverent wonder stems from this confrontation with an unsuspected range of consciousness, the tremendous acceleration of images, the shattering insight into the narrowness of the learned as opposed to the potentiality of awareness, the humbling sense of where one's ego is in relationship to the total energy field.

(a)   I was delighted to see that my skin was dissolving in tiny particles and floating away. I felt as though my outer shell was disintegrating and the "essence" of me was being liberated to join the "essence" of everything else about me.

(b)   Two related feelings were present. One was a tremendous freedom to experience, to be I. It became very important to distinguish between "I" and "Me," the latter being an object defined by patterns and structures and responsibilities—all of which had vanished—and the former being the subject experiencing and feeling. My normal life seemed to be all Me, all demands and responsibilities, a crushing burden which destroyed the pleasure and freedom of being "I." Later in the

13. Campbell, R., "The Circuits of the Senses," in a series on "The Human Body" (Part IV), in *Life*, 54, no. 27 (June 27, 1963), 64–76b.

evening the question of how to fit back into my normal life without becoming a slave of its patterns and demands became paramount. The other related feeling was one of isolation. The struggle to preserve my identity went on in loneliness; the "I" cannot be shared or buttressed. The "Me," structured as it is, can be shared, and is in fact what we mean when we talk about "myself," but once it is thus objectified it is no longer I, it has become the known rather than the knower. And LSD seemed to strip away the structure and to leave the knowing process naked—hence the enormous sense of isolation: there was no Me to be communicated.

(c) All this time, for about 2–3 hours, although there was thinking, talking going on, my mind was being used, yet there was no ego . . . . I could with total dispassion examine various relationships that "I" had with parents, friends, parts of "myself," etc. People who walked into the room were accepted with the same serene equanimity that I felt about accepting my own mental products; they were really walking around in my mind.

(d) I was entering into another dimension of existence. "I" was not. Everything was totally dissolved into a flow of matter continuously moving. No time, no space. A feeling of color, but indescribable. Feeling of movement mainly. Awareness that I, the others, are only collections of clusters of molecules, which are all part of the same stream.

For the small percentage of unprepared subjects who take LSD in careless or manipulative settings and experience terror and paranoid panic, their misery invariably centers around the struggle to reimpose ego control on the whirling energy flow in them and around them. Theirs is the exhausting and sad task of attempting to slow down and limit the electrical pulse of the ten-billion-cell cerebral computer. Thorazine, alcohol and narcotics help apply the brakes. So, I fear, do words.

When we read about the current findings of the energy sciences such as those I have just reviewed, how can our reaction be other than reverent awe at the grandeur of these observations, at the staggering complexity of the design, the speed, the scope? Ecstatic humility before such Power and Intelligence. Indeed, what a small, secular concept—intelligence—to describe that Infinitude of Harmonious Complexity! How impoverished our vocabulary and how narrow our imagination!

Of course, the findings of the pure sciences *do not* produce the religious reaction we should expect. We are satiated with secular statistics, dazed into robot dullness by the enormity of facts which we are not educated to comprehend. Although the findings of physics, genetics, paleontology and neurology have tremendous relevance to our life, they are of less interest than a fall in the stock market or the status of the pennant race.

The message is dimly grasped hypothetically, rationally, but never experienced, felt, known. But there can be that staggering, intellectual-game ecstasy which comes when you begin to sense the complexity of the Plan. To pull back the veil and see for a second a fragment of the energy dance, the life power. How can you appreciate the Divine unless you comprehend the smallest part of the fantastic design? To experience (it's always for a moment) the answers to the four basic spiritual questions is to me the peak of the religious-scientific quest.

But how can our ill-prepared nervous systems grasp the message? Certainly the average man cannot master the conceptual, mathematical bead game of the physics graduate student. Must his experiential contact with the Divine Process come in watered-down symbols, sermons, hymns, robot rituals, religious calendar art, moral-behavior sanctions eventually secular in their aim? Fortunately the Great Plan has produced a happy answer and has endowed every human being with the equipment to comprehend, to know, to experience directly, incontrovertibly. It's there in that network of ten billion cells, the number of whose interconnections "is far greater than all the atoms in the universe."

If you can, for the moment, throw off the grip of your learned mind, your tribal concepts, and experience the message contained in the ten-billion-tube computer which you carry behind your forehead, you would know the awe-full truth. Our research suggests that even the uneducated layman can experience directly what is slowly deduced by scientists—for example physicists, whose heavy, conceptual minds lumber along at three concepts a second, attempting to fathom the speed-of-light processes which their beautiful machines record and which their beautiful symbols portray.

But the brakes can be released. Our recent studies support the hypothesis that psychedelic foods and drugs, ingested by prepared subjects in a serious, sacred, supportive atmosphere, can put the subject in perceptual touch with other levels of energy exchanges.

Remember the data—the Good Friday study, the Savage study, the 69 religious professionals. Forty to ninety percent telling us they experienced "a greater awareness of God, or a Higher Power, or an Ultimate Reality."

But to what do these LSD subjects refer when they report spiritual reactions? Do they obtain specific illuminations into the four basic questions, or are their responses simply awe and wonder at the experienced novelty? Even if the latter were the cause, could it not support the religious application of the psychedelic substances and simply underline the need for more sophisticated religious language coordinated with the scientific data? But there is some evidence, phenomenological but yet haunting, that the spiritual insights accompanying the psychedelic experience might be subjective accounts of the objective findings of astronomy, physics, biochemistry, and neurology.

Now the neurological and pharmacological explanations of an LSD vision are still far from being understood. We know almost nothing about the physiology of consciousness and the body-cortex interaction. We cannot assert that LSD subjects are directly experiencing what particle physicists and biochemists measure, but the evidence about the detailed complexity of the genetic code and the astonishing design of intra-cellular communication should caution us against labeling experiences outside of our current tribal cliches as "psychotic" or abnormal. For three thousand years our greatest prophets and philosophers have been telling us to look within, and today our scientific data are supporting that advice with a humiliating finality. The limits of introspective awareness may well be sub-microscopic, cellular, molecular and even nuclear. We only see, after all, what we are trained and predisposed to see. One of our current research projects involves teaching subjects to recognize internal physical processes much as we train a beginning biology student to recognize events viewed through his microscope.

No matter how parsimonious our explanations, we must accept the fact that LSD subjects do claim to experience revelations into the basic questions and do attribute life-change to their visions.

We are, of course, at the very beginning of our research into these implications. A new experiential language and perhaps even new metaphors for the Great Plan will develop. We have been working on this project for the past two years, writing manuals which train subjects to recognize energy processes, teaching subjects to communicate via a machine we call the experiential typewriter, and with movies of microbiological processes. And we have continued to pose the question to religious and philosophic groups as I am doing tonight. What do you think? Are these biochemical visions religious?

Before you answer, remember that God (however you define the Higher Power) produced that wonderful molecule, that extraordinarily powerful organic substance we call LSD, just as surely as "He" created the rose, or the sun, or the complex cluster of molecules you insist on calling your "self."

Among the many harassing complications of our research into religious experience has been the fact that few people, even some theological professionals, have much conception of what a religious experience really is. Few have any idea how the Divine Process presents Itself. If asked, they tend to become embarrassed, intellectual, evasive. The adored cartoonists of the Renaissance portray the Ultimate Power as a Dove, or a Flaming Bush, or as a man— venerable, with a white beard, or on a Cross, or as a Baby, or a Sage seated in the Full Lotus Position. Are these not incarnations, temporary housings, of the Great Energy Process?

Last fall a minister and his wife, as part of a courageous and dedicated pursuit of illumination, took a psychedelic biochemical called dimethyltryptamine. This wondrous alkaloid (which closely approximates serotonin, the natural "lubricant" of our higher nervous system) produces the most intense psychedelic effect of any sacramental food or drug. In 25 minutes (about the duration of the average sermon), you are whirled through the energy dance, the cosmic process, at the highest psychedelic speed. The 25 minutes are sensed as lasting for a second and for a billion-year Kalpa. After the session, the minister complained that the experience, although shattering and revelatory, was disappointing because it was "content-free"—so physical, so unfamiliar, so scientific, like being beamed through microscopic panoramas, like being oscillated through cellular functions at radar acceleration. Well, what do you expect? If God were to take you on a visit through His "workshop," do you think you'd walk or go by bus? Do you really think it would be a stroll through a celestial Madame Tussaud waxworks? Dear friends, the *Divine Product* is evident in every macroscopic form, in every secular event. The Divine Product we can see. But the *Divine Process* operates in time dimensions which are far beyond our routine, secular, space-time limits. Wave vibrations, energy dance, cellular transactions. Our science describes this logically. Our brains may be capable of dealing with these processes experientially.

So here we are. The Great Process has placed in our hands a key to this direct visionary world. Is it hard for us to accept that the key might be an organic molecule and not a new myth or a new word?

And where do we go? There are in the United States today several hundred thousand persons who have experienced what I have attempted to describe to you tonight—a psychedelic, religious revelation. There are, I would estimate, several million equally thoughtful people who have heard the joyous tidings and who are waiting patiently but determinedly for their psychedelic moment to come.

There is, of course, the expected opposition. The classic conflict of the religious drama—always changing, always the same. The doctrine (which was originally someone's experience) now threatened by the *new* experience. This time the administrators have assigned the inquisitorial role to the psychiatrists, whose proprietary claims to a revealed understanding of the mind and whose antagonism to consciousness-expansion are well known to you.

The clamor over psychedelic drugs is now reaching full crescendo. You have heard rumors and you have read the press assaults and the slick-magazine attacks-by-innuendo. As sophisticated adults you have perhaps begun to wonder: why the hysterical outcry? As scientists you are beginning to ask: where is the evidence? As educated men with an eye for history, you are, I trust, beginning to suspect that we've been through this many times before.

In the current hassle over psychedelic plants and drugs, you are witnessing a good-old-fashioned, traditional, religious controversy. On the one side the psychedelic visionaries, somewhat uncertain about the validity of their revelations, embarrassedly speaking in new tongues (there never is, you know, the satisfaction of a sound, right academic language for the new vision of the Divine), harassed by the knowledge of their own human frailty, surrounded by the inevitable legion of eccentric would-be followers looking for a new panacea, always in grave doubt about their own motivation—(hero? martyr? crank? crackpot?)—always on the verge of losing their material achievements—(job, reputation, long-suffering wife, conventional friends, parental approval); always under the fire of the power-holders. And on the other side: the establishment (the administrators, the police, the fund-granting foundations, the job-givers) pronouncing their familiar lines in the drama: "Danger! Madness! Unsound! Intellectual corruption of youth! Irreparable damage! Cultism!" The issue of chemical expansion of consciousness is hard upon us. During the next months, every avenue of propaganda is going to barrage you with the arguments. You can hardly escape it. You are going to be pressed for a position. Internal Freedom is becoming a major religious and civil-rights controversy.

How can you decide? How can you judge? Well, it's really quite simple. Whenever you hear anyone sounding off on internal freedom and consciousness-expanding foods and drugs—whether pro or con —check out these questions:

(1) Is your advisor talking from direct experience, or simply repeating cliches? Theologians and intellectuals often deprecate "experience" in favor of fact and concept. This classic debate is falsely labeled. Most often it becomes a case of "experience" versus "inexperience."

(2) Do his words spring from a spiritual or from a mundane point of view? Is he motivated by a dedicated quest for answers to basic questions, or is he protecting his own social-psychological position, his own game investment?

(3) How would his argument sound if it were heard in a different culture (for example, in an African jungle hut, a ghat on the Ganges, or on another planet inhabited by a form of life superior to ours); or in a different time (for example in Periclean Athens, or in a Tibetan monastery, or in a bull-session led by any one of the great religious leaders—founders—messiahs); or how would it sound to other species of life on our planet today—to the dolphins, to the consciousness of a redwood tree? In other words, try to break out of your usual tribal game-set and listen with the ears of another one of God's creatures.

(4) How would the debate sound to you if you were fatally diseased with a week to live, and thus less committed to mundane issues? Our research group receives many requests a week for consciousness-expanding experiences, and some of these come from terminal patients.[14]

(5) Is the point of view one which opens up or closes down?

14. The medical press has recently reported on the analgesic use of LSD with terminal cancer patients. Cf. *Medical World News*, August 30, 1963; *Medical Tribune*, April 8, 1963; and *J. Amer. Med. Assoc.*, January 4, 1964.

Are you being urged to explore, experience, gamble out of spiritual faith, join someone who shares your cosmic ignorance on a collaborative voyage of discovery? Or are you being pressured to close off, protect your gains, play it safe, accept the authoritative voice of someone who knows best?

(6) When we speak, we say little about the subject-matter and disclose mainly the state of our own mind. Does your psychedelic advisor use terms which are positive, pro-life, spiritual, inspiring, opening, based on faith in the future, faith in your potential, or does he betray a mind obsessed by danger, material concern, by imaginary terrors, administrative caution or essential distrust in your potential. Dear friends, there is nothing in life to fear, no spiritual game can be lost. The choice is not double-bind but double-win.[15]

(7) If he is against what he calls "artificial methods of illumination," ask him what constitutes the natural. Words? Rituals? Tribal customs? Alkaloids? Psychedelic vegetables?

(8) If he is against biochemical assistance, where does he draw the line? Does he use nicotine? alcohol? penicillin? vitamins? conventional sacramental substances?

(9) If your advisor is against LSD, what is he for? If he forbids you the psychedelic key to revelation, what does he offer you instead?

SUMMARY

The outline of this paper can be summarized as follows:

(1) Evidence is cited that, depending on the set and setting, from 40 to 90 percent of psychedelic subjects report intense religious experiences.

(2) The religious experience was defined as the ecstatic, incontrovertibly certain, subjective discovery of answers to four basic questions which concern ultimate power and design, life, man and self. It was pointed out that science attempts to provide objective, external answers to these same questions.

(3) We considered the hypothesis that the human being might be able to become directly aware of energy exchanges and biological processes for which we now have no language and no perceptual training. Psychedelic foods and drugs were suggested as one key to

15. Levitsky, A., personal communication.

these neurological potentials, and subjective reports from LSD sessions were compared with current findings from the energy sciences.

(4) The current controversy over the politics of the nervous system (which involves secular-external versus spiritual-internal commitments) were reviewed, and a checklist for the intelligent voter was presented.

PSYCHEDELICS & RELIGION: A SYMPOSIUM

Raziel Abelson, Allen Ginsberg, & Michael Wyschogrod

INTRODUCTION: RAZIEL ABELSON

THE PURPOSE OF THIS SYMPOSIUM IS TO DISCUSS THE RELIGIOUS AND philosophical aspects of the so-called "consciousness expanding" drugs, particularly LSD and marijuana. It occurs to me that the title of this symposium is much too pretentious and stuffy; I would prefer to call it something simpler and more cozy. I suggest we call this a "Trip-in," for a reason not quite what you would naturally think. My reason is a personal one: it has to do with various trips I have made recently and a new one I am reluctant to take until I can see a good reason for it.

I am particularly interested in the subject of our discussion because of my feeling of closeness to the generation that has made it an issue, the generation that came of age or will come of age in the 1960's. I consider it an extraordinarily interesting generation, the most exciting that I have had contact with. My own generation of the 40's was, I think, not a bad one; it was interested in its fellowmen,

"Psychedelics and Religion: A Symposium." From *The Humanist*, Fall 1967. Reprinted by permission of the publisher.

The following article, edited by Raziel Abelson, is drawn from a symposium on drugs held in 1967 at New York University. The primary purpose of this article, as described by Abelson, "is to discuss the religious and philosophical aspects of the so-called 'consciousness expanding' drugs." Allen Ginsberg argues the value of using hallucinogenic drugs in seeking a more intense religious experience, while Michael Wyschogrod describes drug use, in a religious context, as an attempt to develop instant mysticism. Wyschogrod's argument is not based on the morality or legality of drug use, but on the artificiality of religious experience stemming from psychedelic drugs. Abelson provides, in his post mortem, a very careful critique of the positions taken by Ginsberg and Wyschogrod.

it was dynamic and hard working, it fought a world war against barbarism, but it was not as free as the present one because it was enslaved to ideologies. For the conservative prejudices of our parents we substituted the radical and neo-Puritanical prejudices of Marxism and Freudianism. I began to teach in the 1950's, and the generation of students who attended my lectures in that decade was, I think, the dullest, most boring of my time. It was enslaved to things far worse than ideologies: to chrome-plated Cadillacs, large houses, good jobs and social status. Its heroes were McCarthy on the "right" and Eisenhower on the "left." I first began to enjoy teaching in the 60's, because only then did I feel a rapport with students, whom I found so remarkably free that I felt myself liberated by them—free of pretentious ideology, free of mechanical rules of grammar, spelling, etiquette and sexual behavior, free of parental authoritarianism, of superstitions and phobias, willing to explore and appreciate any kind of human experience, able to say, like Marsiglio of Padua: "Nothing human is alien to me." Unfortunately, my age disqualifies me from full, card-carrying membership in this new generation, but, unlike Lewis Feuer and Ronald Reagan, I recognize its superiority to my own and I would like to be at least an honorary or associate member. For this reason, I have tried to share its experience by taking various "trips" with it. In 1963 I took a trip on a rickety old school bus at four in the morning, to the Washington March for civil rights legislation. The following summer I took a trip to Mississippi to observe the Freedom Schools and voter registration drive; although I wasn't there long, I did get a taste of the "agony and the ecstasy" of the students who fought non-violently and valiantly for reason and decency. I believe that summer of 1964 was the most glorious moment in the history of American youth; it was the moment at which the older generations began to look to the youth for the leadership they did not have the courage to assume. Two summers later I took another trip on a rickety old school bus, full of students, to march on Washington to end the war in Viet Nam, and this year I marched with them in New York, surrounded by Viet Cong banners and hippies with bananas, flowers, and electric guitars. Up to that point, the generation of the 60's had always turned me on. Their skeptical rebelliousness and their intense social involvement seemed to me to promise a far better world when they would take control. But something very disturbing has been happening in the last two years. This generation, that created in me and many others so much hope for the future, has itself lost hope and nerve, and has turned from social concern inward toward its own private experience: it has turned from iconoclasm to quietism, from humanistic liberalism to passivity and drugs. The revolutionary generation is "copping out."

The "trips" I had taken with it were all outward, other-centered, and to get things done that needed doing. Now, if I listen to the proselytes of Liberation Through Drugs, I am to take a trip in the exact opposite direction—inward, toward passivity, hallucination, inconsequence. Maybe I can understand the motives for this shift into reverse gear—disappointment at the snail's pace of social reforms, moral revulsion and despair about the abominable, uncontrollable and endless war in Viet Nam—but motives are not reasons, and I would like to know the *reason* why, before I take this trip backward into darkness. I am in search of enlightenment: why are drug induced fantasies better than the light of cool reason; why is sensual over-stimulation more worthwhile than the pursuit of rational social ideals? I look to two extremely well-qualified experts to enlighten me on these questions. From Mr. Ginsberg I hope for a clear answer to the question, "Why?" and from Professor Wyschogrod, an equally clear explanation of "Why not?"

TURNING ON WITH LSD & POT: ALLEN GINSBERG

I would like to begin by introducing some data from comparative religion. Those who have done any dilettanting around in Tantric Hinduism or its esoteric erotic sexual practices will no doubt know of the book, *The Serpent Power*, by Arthur Avalon. It is a translation of an ancient Hindu text, the *Mahanirvana tantra*, one of the older, more conservative texts of the Shaivite school of Hinduism. This text deals with ritual, prayer, and the formal religious use of marijuana. If one reads just a few sentences from the text, he can get an appreciation of the importance of the use of marijuana in the religious rituals. One who engages in mantra prayer and chanting will use this narcotic hemp in his ceremonies.

I should point out that I am a formally initiated member of the Shiva sect, and I assume that my presentation of its rituals is protected by the First Amendment of the U. S. Constitution. Since I have a central preoccupation within my heart with religious matters, I wish to stay off legal problems and to focus upon the actual subject matter on a more realistic level, without worrying about whether it's going to be against the law, whether it's moral or immoral to break the law, whether you'll go mad or you won't go mad. I want to deal with the phenomenology of LSD and pot and their philosophical implications. Professor Elia Rubichek of Prague, who has done a lot of work on LSD, defines it in Pavlovian and Marxian terminology, the terminology the "Iron Curtain" would use in dealing with the effects of LSD. The phraseology is really interesting. What he said was, "It inhibits conditioned reflexes." Now that's a big deal out there in Russia where there's a Pavlovian conception of consciousness, because it means that there is a way of reversing or wiping out the conditioning that would make a member of the former upper class no longer eligible to be condemned by the bureaucrat. Anybody could take LSD and say that he had his conditioned reflexes wiped out and was now just as good as the proletariat.

What it means in terms of our country is something you have been digging lately—Marshall McLuhan's generalizations about the effects of the conditioning of our technology on our consciousness. He's saying that the media or environment we have created around us is a giant conditioning mechanism, a giant teaching machine. We are hardly aware of it as a teaching machine. We are hardly aware of its effect. We are hardly aware that consciousness is not necessarily a conceptual or verbal matter, that there are other levels of consciousness, depths of consciousness, that there is feeling consciousness, that there is touch consciousness, that there is smelling, seeing, hearing, and levels of memory consciousness that we are not generally aware of. But McLuhan has been saying recently that the verbal and language consciousness that we have been conditioned to over the last centuries has atrophied our other senses. That is, the universe into which we have projected ourselves and developed has atrophied our other sense—smell, touch, taste—in a way that he could even quantify. McLuhan told me that he wanted to work out a way to quantify in scientific terminology the difference caused by our preoccupation with visual consciousness; that is, the difference caused to the other senses. There is a quantitative mode of measurement that he could apply. What has this to do with LSD? McLuhan didn't know the connection because he hasn't taken LSD or read much about it. Yet given a chemical which can reverse conditioning, we have a kind of open consciousness which receives almost all of the data present to us and takes account of it all, as if that which we usually are not aware of or is unconscious within us is presented to our awareness during the time that we are high on LSD. This goes on without any screening structure—something that Leary has been saying over and over—to the point where something is either understood and is boring or is not understood and is still a koan for people to solve.

What good is that kind of consciousness? I don't know if I have presented it clearly enough to have any value for you. It involves a consciousness that is not socially conditioned (though conditioned by our bodies surely), a consciousness where the social conditioning is reversed, and where we had eight hours to look around us as new-born babes to see our bodies, to see our relationships, to see our architecture around us, to see our relationships to other forms of life. It involves eight hours of experience of ourselves as mammalian sentient beings. Is that a socially useful experience?

I think it always has been considered a socially useful experience. I think that the LSD experience approximates the mystical experience, as it is called, the religious experience, or the peak experience, as Maslow calls it. It approximates the kind of experience that one reads about in William James's *The Varieties of Religious Experience*. I'm not sure it's identical with what people would call the classical religious experience, but then in William James one also finds that very few of those experiences are identical experiences. Their common quality is that there is a break in the normal mode of consciousness, an opening up of another universe of awareness, so that from one description to another in any of the books describing mystical experiences the forms are not the same. One thing that everybody cries out in delight at is that the universe they had taken for granted had suddenly opened and revealed itself as something much deeper and fuller, much more exquisite, something more connected with a divine sense of things—a Self perhaps. So I would say that the LSD experience does approximate what we humans have been recording over millenia as a flight of higher imagination or a flight of higher awareness. Now that experience has always been accorded a very honored status in society. A few people have been burned at the stake or crucified for attempting to manifest the insights that they've experienced. But at least in the academies, in religion, in the church, and even among truck drivers, there is a respect for the non-conditioned, non-verbal, non-conceptual opening up of the mind to all of the data of experience flooding in at once, newly perceived, or perceived as a newborn babe or early child.

Its usefulness in our society is extra. That's why I began talking about McLuhan, inasmuch as we have arrived at sort of a Buck Rogers space age, science-fiction society in which everybody is electronically intercommunicated, in which visual images and verbal images are multiplied, stereotyped and implanted in everybody's brain so that it is very difficult to escape the automatic, mechanistic forms that are constantly being played on our bodies by radio, television, newspapers, by our own university, or by our own parents.

In a world now facing apocalypse, in the sense that America, the largest world power, is perhaps preparing for a war on the Asiatic life form, it becomes important not only to see what we have in common with the Asiatic life form and what we actually have distinct and separate from it but also to find those points, to control the angers built up in us, to measure the actual universe around, to lose the conditioning that brought us to this path of anger, fear and paranoia, to experience what is original in our nature as distinct from what has been educated into our nature since our birth. The problem, however, that still arises, particularly when people have had religious experience and have not had LSD experience, is this question: "Is this experience like an evil specter or is it something that can be reconciled with the older religious experience? Does it have any relationship to the norms of human experience, or at least the high norms of human experience, that are described in the religious books?

Of these we have neither enough experiments nor enough data. My own experience is as follows: When I was younger (when I was about 28) I had a series of visionary or religious or illuminative experiences which are best categorized as the aesthetic experience, since they became catalyzed by reading poems of Blake. I had an auditory hallucination of Blake's voice and also experienced a number of moments of guilelessness about the world around me and feeling that the father of the universe had existed all along but I had not realized it, that the father of the universe loved me and that I was identical with the father. So this was an experience of bliss. I realized that I had my place in the universe. I tried to describe this a few times in poetry or in prose but it's very difficult to describe. At the time that I had it (it was about in 1948) this kind of experience was, at least in the circles where I ran (Columbia University), an experience which was practically unknown and was considered madness. I remember that when this happened I went to Lionel Trilling and said, "I've seen light." And he looked at me and seemed to be wondering, "What am I going to do with this?" He looked as if he wondered where I was going to wind up. There were two people at Columbia at the time who had enough inner experience to be able to understand, to talk to me, to reassure me. One was Raymond Weaver who had been the first biographer for Herman Melville and who had lived in Japan and was for those at Columbia in the forties *the* great light, a secret light because he was a cranky cat. He used to know Hart Crane and Wanda Landowska. He was the most eminent professor at Columbia. He shared an office with Mark Van Doren. Weaver could deal with this kind of experience without slipping out and becoming anxious. Mark Van Doren also could deal with it. When I went to him in an overexcited and totally disoriented state and said, "I have seen some light, I heard Blake's voice!" he said, "What kind of light was it?" Then he began questioning me about the quality of the experience, asking for data. Everybody else thought I was nuts. However I am what I am. So I'll stand in my own body and believe my own senses and experiences.

Later I found that LSD catalyzed a variety of consciousness that was very similar to the natural experience. I've used a variety of other hallucinogenics—maybe about thirty times over a fifteen-year period. This is very small actually compared to the usage now being made by the younger people. I found that there has not been any contradiction between the kind of consciousness I had under LSD and my height of rapture of consciousness in natural moments. I also found that I faced the same difficulties with LSD as I had faced with my original visionary experience. Those difficulties were that, having gotten into a state of high perception, how to maintain my normal life, my awareness on a higher level, incorporating in my daily experience some of the concrete perceptions that I had in a moment of ecstasy. Specifically I had had a non-drug vision in the Columbia book store. I'd gone in there for years, and I went in there this day and suddenly I saw that everybody looked like tortured animals. I was reading Blake's poem about—

> I wander through London's chartered streets
> Near where the chartered Thames doth flow
> On every face I meet I see
> Marks of weakness
> Marks of woe

Well, in those moments I saw marks of suffering on the faces of the bookstore clerks, the enormous-like mammalism sexual deliciousness of their being and the contrary stultified, rigid, unsexualized, non-feeling, day-to-day commerce over the books with a few camp jokes mixed in to refer to the unknown. I asked, How, in coming down to a day-to-day dealing with the bookstore people or anyone on the campus, how to deal with such persons, such deep persons as exist in everybody? And that took very slow practice and continuous awareness of the fact that everyone was a deep person and a divine mammal rather than a bookstore clerk. The same problem exists in relation to LSD. Having had a vision on LSD of either your parents' or your own role, how do you manifest that in your school life or whatever life you are pursuing? Henri Michaud, a great French poet who did a lot of early experiments, finally told me that he had concluded that what was important was not the visions, but what people did with the visions afterward, and how they manifested them in their daily life. I think that the really basic practical problem to be faced is the problem common to all mysticism. How is one in day-to-day life to keep continuous high consciousness of the eternal which he had experienced in separated moments of a larger consciousness? What good is it if they are separated moments; if they are not totally, distinctly integrated into every day life? Having experienced only separated moments of divine consciousness without drugs, I find that the drugs do make possible a return to more native awareness which is useful when I have to take stock of my activities. For instance, a year and a half ago I was involved in the Viet-Nam Day Committee in Berkeley. There was a great deal of anger and outrage about the war. I found myself being swept along into that outrage and vowing vengeance on the murderers of innocent children; and my wits were astray because of all of that senseless tumult; and I all but cried for vengeance on the murderers. I took some LSD the day the President went for his gall bladder operation and I realized that he was another suffering deep person, perhaps one almost ignorant of his own state of consciousness and so suffering a great deal more because of that ignorance, one however entering the valley of the shadow. My hatred simply disappeared. What was left was a funny kind of compassion for him in his ignorance, a prayer for him for his return from the valley of the shadow. In a state of awareness, less hostile, less fearful, less paranoid than his entrance, I found myself praying for him, praying for his own understanding. The thing that I did realize was that my piling up my own hatred on top of the general hatred of the Pentagon and the *New York Daily News* and the military and industrial complex only added to the anti-Vietnam War reaction. Piling up my hatred and my curses and my magic on top of that was going to make the situation worse. I wanted to move to liquidate the anger hallucination that was controlling everybody.

Finally, we have a few other details that might interest you. A poet friend of mine has worked for ten years in Zen monasteries, has done formal meditation, and is an accomplished Zen student. He was here in America a few months ago, and we had several conversations about the rising LSD culture and the Haight-Ashburys. He felt that the LSD experience was not contradictory to the experience of Satori as described by Zen. The younger, qualified, completely trained Zen masters in Japan who had tried LSD were interested in it and considered it a useful tool for education in relation to their own discipline. They were not against its use and were themselves beginning to employ it. The Roshi Suzuki—Roshi means master—who is the head of the meditation sect in San Francisco, said he felt the LSD experience is not the same as Zazen sitting meditation. However he finds that most of the meditators in his group are people who are originally turned on by LSD. As far as he can see, it does open people up to a widening area of consciousness, which can then be worked in with other disciplines. I find the same report coming in now from the schools of Tibetan Buddhism. There is a Geshe who has a monastery in New Jersey. He has some American disciples who have been equally experienced in Tibetan meditation and psychedelics. Wanga and his disciple, Tenjin, who is an ex-Harvard student, have prepared translations of old Tibetan meditation texts and are preparing them for publication with the foreword note that the Tibetan prayers, methods and procedures may be found useful in collaboration with psychedelic experiments. Thus it seems clear to me that there is a close relationship between psychedelic drugs and mystical experience.

INSTANT MYSTICISM:
MICHAEL WYSCHOGROD

I think the point of view expressed by Allen Ginsberg is a very good one—an attitude of reason, of peace, of affection, of understanding, and therefore, I am not in a polemical spirit. I do not wish to disagree, to forbid, to outlaw, or to consider LSD and marijuana evil or immoral. They exist like many other things in the world, and it's very superficial to take a simple "no" attitude to what one finds in the world.

Nevertheless there are a number of issues that deserve deeper analysis. I think the two issues we do not want to discuss are these: first, I think it a mistake to approach this problem from the point of view of the dangers involved. The dangers, of course, are not irrelevant. I think anyone who contemplates taking psychedelic drugs deserves to have all of the knowledge necessary so that he can make an intelligent choice as to just what risk is involved; but that is not a final word because many things in life involve risk and yet we don't shun them. In this country the automobile kills forty thousand people a year, and yet I have not heard anyone advocate the abolition of the automobile. For some reason we feel that the advantages of the automobile outweigh the disadvantages. In any case if the psychedelic substances have substantial spiritual and religious advantages, then I would be prepared to say that this outweighs a great many perils and disadvantages. So the element of peril, though relevant, in my opinion is not crucial and is not the final consideration. Secondly, I think that this problem ought not to be approached essentially from the legal point of view, because whether we ought or ought not to outlaw something is again a secondary question.

The first consideration is, is this a good thing or a bad thing? Outlawing is only secondary. Even if we decide that this is a bad thing, it does not necessarily follow that it ought to be outlawed. The heart of the matter is the question: what good are these drugs? And the moment we ask this question we are in the religious realm. My thesis can be stated very simply: it's a thesis of wonder and surprise. I find that the younger generation to which Professor Abelson referred senses that there is something wrong with the technological mode of existence into which we have been projected in the middle of the twentieth century. There is something wrong with the artificiality of our existence. We no longer experience reality. We live through artificial media such as the television and radio, which have a life of their own and stand as a screen between man and reality. Life in our times is in essence artificial. And because it is artificial there are those people who want to break through this artificiality on all levels, who want to live as a man ought to live and was intended to live, in serenity and peace, with direct contact with reality, not in a life of instant coffee, instant pudding, instant bake mixes, and instant this and that and the other thing—but a wholesale life of cooking vegetables as they grow and taking flour and using it for baking, of brewing coffee, instead of getting it out of an instant mix. Our lives are nightmares of instant experiences. And this, of course, is a profound truth. But then something amazing has happened and I am genuinely amazed—suddenly there is instant mysticism, there is technological mysticism, instead of patience, serenity, humility and waiting for enlightenment and praying for it and loving our fellow man. Instead we look to chemistry: "better living through better things through chemistry."

It seems to me that the genuinely religious person cannot want to buy his relationship to God in a sugar cube, a bottle, or a chemical. It is true that these substances are not yet mass-produced by the pharmaceutical companies. But perhaps that won't take long, if this thing catches on and if people go for it. I assure you that in a few years *Life* and *Time* will be full of ads and every drug company will be selling the stuff and holding out the hope of a quick road to God. And there will be competition, there will be the jingles. I don't want that. I think that would be a travesty on genuine religion, genuine mysticism, and genuine religious experience.

The real thing is always harder and more difficult to achieve than the imitation. And with the real thing you run the risk of never quite making it. There is one element and thought that is universally agreed on among scholars of religion, and that is this: there is a profound distinction between magic and religion. The distinction is simple: Magic is power; religion is prayer. The magician is of the opinion that there is some secret formula which, when discovered, gives him power over the spirit. Once he has that, the spirit cannot refuse his demands. The spirit of magic and the spirit of modern technology are very close indeed because both see man in the driver's seat. Both see man as the power that controls the world around him, and human destiny as a destiny with ever greater control over human existence. Just as through technology we control our environment, the heat and the cold, and the world around us, so by means of magic was the same attempted. The only difference was that we think that science works better than magic. But the spirit is the same; and against science and against magic stands genuine religion. Genuine religion is prayer. Prayer is asking God, and he can say "no."

There is the story of the little kid who prayed; and his cynical uncle said, "Well God didn't answer you, did he?" And the little kid answered, "Yes, he did. He said, 'No.'"

This is the spirit of true religion. In genuine religion we hand ourselves over to the greater spirit, whether one calls it "God," "the Father," or "the spirit of the universe." Fundamentally it doesn't matter. But you see yourself as worshipping that being, that spirit, loving Him. He loves you in return. And you live in peace and union with Him.

Drug mysticism is the conversion of mysticism into magic. It is the illusion that can can have power over the spirit; and this never has happened and never will happen. What comes in a bottle or in a chemical is not the spirit of God. What comes in a bottle or a chemical is an illusion. It is the epitome of just that technological threat against which well-meaning people are fighting and succumbing to through drugs and narcotics. It is the victory of the slogan of the chemical industry, and I don't want to see that happen.

GINSBERG REPLIES TO WYSCHOGROD

For all I know perhaps Professor Wyschogrod is right! I have no idea about the victory of the chemical industry, or victory of artificial madness, or black magic technology. Burroughs, a former teacher of mine and someone I respect a great deal, has had considerable experience with hallucinogens and has stopped using them. Occasionally he turns on; but lately he has taken to saying, "No, I'd better watch out. The Pentagon is going to poison us all. Things have gotten too Orwellian."

As to religious reality, I don't agree with Professor Wyschogrod as to what constitutes a valid religious experience. The spirit of religion is investigation and practice, of which prayer is only an element. But there isn't a pre-supposition, or what I call a hang-up on a Jehovah, that you've got up there that you've got to be humble to, that you've got to pray to, or to be said "no" by. Jehovah is within in Buddhism and Hinduism and in some aspects of Christianity and actually in some Hebraic traditions also. The external Jehovah is just high camp. In some schools that sense of an external authority is not relied on, certainly not in Buddhism where one of the major koans is that Buddha is not a divine being to be worshipped. The saying is that, "If you meet the Buddha on the way to enlightenment and he bars your way, cut him down!"

As to LSD coming in a bottle and whether or not it is the spirit of God, it all depends on the way we are using the term "god." If there were a Jehovah I wouldn't put it past him to come through a bottle any way. Certainly it would be within his power. Certainly a God would see it as equally charming to come through a bottle as through prayer. So I don't think there is anything to be feared in that sense. What might be feared is dependence on the drug and lack of ritual or lack of prayer or lack of humility or lack of earnestness in the yoga of the drug. I tried to provide the suggestions for ritual, the suggestions for prayer, the suggestions for the application of the drug vision to daily life. But I think that purely verbal terminologies are a bit over-dramatized in speaking of LSD as merely "magic" as opposed to religion. I think those are verbal distinctions. I think they are basically stereotypes of thought. I don't think they fit the enormity and eloquence of the experience which many of us have felt.

WYSCHOGROD REPLIES TO GINSBERG

I agree with Mr. Ginsberg that these are very serious matters and it's presumptuous for anyone to say what is the case and what is not the case. Yet each of us talks from his own experience. I do not speak out of LSD experience but I talk out of religious experience and I think that I am reporting what I see. I don't think that I have the last word. I don't think that I am right, but do feel deeply that there is profound danger here.

I would add just one word. I don't know much about eastern religion. I deeply respect it. I have an intuitive sense that there is something very real and very deep there, but I'm not a Japanese, Chinese or a Far Easterner. I'm a Westerner. What goes on in the Far East in the setting of that civilization over the thousands of years of art, poetry, and history, and what has gone into the development of those religions I cannot enter into. Therefore I think it is spiritually dangerous for men of New York, for example, to take one aspect of foreign or eastern civilization and transport it here and to think that we have the same thing here that they have. We are Jews or Christians and there is very much to Judaism and Christianity, and we must be what we are. I think there is something very sad about a person trying to be something that he is not and never can be.

Mr. Ginsberg advises people to take pot and LSD. Now I grant an individual the full freedom to act as he wishes and to be what he wishes and I'd be the last person to take that away. But at the same time I must express my convictions. Life poses a peculiar problem: to become what you are. Now this sounds paradoxical, because if you are what you are, why do you need to become what you are? Here there is always tension between becoming what you are, and becoming what you are meant to be. And that's the job for each of us to find. All I can do for you is to say, Look once more before you embark on this strange new path of psychedelic religion. Look once more at your heritage. Just give it a second look and after that you're on your own.

POST MORTEM:
RAZIEL ABELSON

I must confess that I do not feel I have received the enlightenment I had hoped for—I am not exactly in a state of Satori. The trouble with this discussion is that both participants have assumed something to be the case which, it seems to me, is even more doubtful than the qualities of the drugs they have argued about. Both Ginsberg and Wyschogrod have assumed that religious experience is necessarily good, and I do not see any reason for accepting that assumption. Ginsberg has argued that, because religious experience is always good, and (he claims) LSD and marijuana help produce religious experience, these drugs are very good and useful things. Wyschogrod has argued, to the contrary, that drugs cannot *possibly* (later he modified his claim to the effect that they do not, so far as he can see) produce genuine religious experience, but only spurious, synthetic, "instant," "bottled," in a word, *illusory* religious experience. Thus he takes it for granted that there is a clear distinction between illusion and reality in religious experience. On this point, it seems to me, Ginsberg has much the better of the argument. To Wyschogrod's claim "You can't get God out of a bottle" Ginsberg replied, very sensibly, "Why not?"

Why not, indeed? I am reminded of Philip Roth's story, *The Conversion of the Jews,* in which the Rabbi pontificates to his Hebrew school class that Christianity is more irrational than Judaism, because it (Christianity) claims that Jesus was born without sexual intercourse; and little Ozzie then demands to know why an omnipotent God, who can divide the Red Sea and send plagues over

Egypt, cannot make a woman become pregnant without sexual intercourse. Once we begin talking about the transcendental (a fancy word for supernatural) anything goes—each one makes up his own rules. One says you can't find God in a bottle, but you can in a burning bush; another says God can't make a woman pregnant without intercourse but that the Holy Ghost in the form of a dove can. How adjudicate such theological claims, and why bother? How one can find God depends very much on just what one means by "God," and it is not at all clear what either Ginsberg or Wyschogrod means, and still less clear whether whatever they mean exists. And if He doesn't exist, you can no more find Him through prayer than through drugs or in a bottle.

Now it seems to me that the distinction between real and unreal, whether it is applied to religious experience, to God, or to the beauty and goodness allegedly revealed by psychedelic drugs, is crucial to this discussion. And my own objection to the claims made for such drugs is on the philosophical ground that this distinction is being applied to a type of experience to which it cannot properly be applied, because there are no established criteria for making the distinction. Indeed, the experience, being hallucinatory, is such that there cannot possibly be criteria for distinguishing the real from the apparent. Mr. Ginsberg made this clear in describing how, under LSD, he felt compassion for everyone and anything, for President Johnson and (he said to me later) for Adolph Hitler. Now what sense is there in compassion that does not distinguish the executioner from his victims? How can one have real compassion for the sufferer without hating the agent who makes him suffer? What good is such compassion; indeed, is it really compassion, or is this feeling of compassion not as hallucinatory as everything else in the state of being drugged? To be more exact, the trouble here is that there is no objective way of distinguishing what is real from what is imaginary, hallucinatory, apparent, spurious, or in any sense unreal. The psychedelic experience is one that, by its very nature, leads one beyond (or below) all criteria of reality. One can, of course, easily say that it leads one to a "higher reality," but this verbalism is empty because "real" makes no sense where it cannot be distinguished from unreal. And this breakdown of the distinction is, of course, typical of all modes of irrationality, including religious mysticism. Consequently, it is impossible to judge whether psychedelic experience and religious experience are the same or different. All we can say is that they are equally hallucinatory. Why the speakers should assume that that is a very good thing is still a mystery to me.

In effect, Mr. Ginsberg has made two claims: first that psychedelic drugs are good in an instrumental sense because they have beneficial effects on one's personality and abilities, and second, that the experience they induce is intrinsically good. The first claim, it seems to me, cannot be authoritatively established by Mr. Ginsberg or anyone else who testifies only from personal experience, any more than the therapeutic value of psychoanalysis can be established by brainwashed patients who have been persuaded by their analyst that they are much improved (when no one else can see any difference in their behavior). Such a claim can only be proved by carefully controlled scientific studies, and no conclusive studies have yet been made. So I would discount this claim completely, just as anyone with sense would discount the claims made by Krebiozin enthusiasts, and just as Freud came close to discrediting himself as a doctor when he made premature claims for the therapeutic value of cocaine.

The second claim, that the psychedelic experience is intrinsically good, is more difficult to assess, for the reason that its value has to be judged within the experience (I am frequently rebuked by students when I question the value of taking drugs. I am told I haven't tried them, so I can't possibly know whether they are good or bad). Yet the experience is such that within it, all established criteria of good or bad are dissolved, just as, in a dream, the criteria for distinguishing real from apparent cease to apply. One dreams that something is real and something else is not, but this distinction is itself dreamt, and therefore ineffectual. Consequently, it makes no more sense to say that what one experiences is bad than to say that it is good. We simply have no standards for evaluating the hallucinatory objects of a psychedelic experience, for we have no standards for evaluating any hallucinatory objects. So far, the human race is a reality-oriented species. If enough people take drugs, this may change, and then the philosophical premises of a discussion such as this will be different, but it is as useless to speculate on such a state of affairs as to try to imagine what the world would be like if the laws of physics ceased to hold.

I do not mean to question the right of anyone, including Mr. Ginsberg, to express a preference for any type of experience he chooses to enjoy. If someone likes to smoke pot or take acid, and injures no one else in doing so, that, so far as I am concerned, is his affair; and I no more support legislation against such activities than I support legislation against suicide. But to say that one likes something is not the same as to say that that something is good. I do very strongly object to the proselytizing of drugs, because, as I have tried to explain, there are no objective grounds for making a claim either to intrinsic value or to instrumental value with respect to such drugs. I still see one rather compelling reason not to take them, a reason that I tried to indicate in my opening remarks. To steep onself in illusion is to escape from the irksome necessity to distinguish illusion from reality —in a word, to cop out. My conclusion from this discussion is: there's a lot of work to be done in the real world, and a lot of real beauty to enjoy—let's get on with it.

WINDS FROM THE EAST:
YOUTH & COUNTER CULTURE

Jacob Needleman

SEVERAL SERIOUS THINKERS HAVE RECENTLY ATTEMPTED TO UNDERSTAND the new religious mind of young America, and I think what is most instructive about these efforts is the way they have failed. One must hasten to add that the problem is formidably difficult. The turning of our young people to mysticism and Eastern religion is a phenomenon so various and pervasive, and seems to touch on so many sides of the present crisis of civilization, that one may well despair of grasping its true significance. How much is only the flash of youthful rebellion? the love of anything alien at a moment in time when familiar values are drained of their energy? And how many among us are able to distinguish between the real content of these new teachings and what seems to be the extravagance of their followers? We may have one or two thoughts about Zen, for example, but what or who is Meher Baba, Subud, Krishnamurti, Vajrayana Buddhism or Sufism? Are we obliged to try to understand these teachings at their source, or is it enough to pass judgment on the young people who proclaim them?

In a recent article in *The Saturday Review of Literature*, Marcia Cavell, a professor of philosophy at NYU, wove her case against the new religions around the pronouncements of Charles Manson.

> Guilt, as Manson says, is a figment of the imagination. One re-
> members that Satan's greatest snare has always been the promise
> of . . . "paradise now." A lesson to be learned from the Manson
> cult, I think, is that dreams of heaven often pave the road to hell.

"Winds from the East: Youth and Counter Culture," by Jacob Needleman. From *Commonweal*, 94 (April 21, 1972). Copyright © 1972 by Commonweal Publishing Company. The essay appeared originally as "Winds from the East: Youth and Counter-Cults." Reprinted by permission of the publisher.

Elsewhere in her article, she admits that her judgments about Eastern religion are those of a superficial observer, but the clear implication is that one does not need to be more superficial about Eastern teachings to see where they are leading the young.

This is the problem for many of us. It is hard to resist lumping the younger generation's enthusiasm about Oriental religion together with drug abuse, occultism and witchcraft with all of its often childish, bizarre or even heinous applications. John Passmore, another philosopher, writing in *Encounter,* sees this "new mysticism" as little more than a puerile urge for instant gratification and feels no need to cite any writer more penetrating than Timothy Leary. "Zen Buddhism," Passmore claims, "positively prides itself on its moral and political irresponsibility." With that, he hastens to remind us that various Nazis also found their inspiration in "mysticism," and then he notes that

> Contemporary hippy-mystics are often convinced that they are the recipients of a special divine grace. They display that fanaticism, "aristocratic" pride and antinomianism which Wesley so feared, setting themselves above all kinds of moral restraint.

At the other extreme, Charles A. Reich in *The Greening of America* sees this new "consciousness" as the great hope for America and the whole Western world. It offers, he says, "the sensual beauty of a creative, loving unrepressed life." Unlike Christianity, which, according to Reich, has become just another form of future-oriented repression, the ideals of the young are read as a force for a complete and immediate transformation.

Only Theodore Roszak, in *The Making of a Counter Culture,* strikes for a sense of discrimination between the counterfeit answers and real questions that this movement of the young brings to us. It is certainly no criticism of Roszak to say that his approach remains bound to Western psychological and sociological categories; it is his notable achievement to have stayed within those categories and yet to have communicated through them a hard sense of the religious that is new to modern man. But even Roszak leaves us with the understanding that the value of the "mystical" lies in its power to satisfy certain ordinary desires of men.

None of these writers ever seriously questions his own understanding of the nature and function of religious training. Yet to provoke such questioning can be the most immediately significant result of the so-called "spiritual revolution." Without this self-questioning, we shall continue to be so fascinated by passing judgment on the young that we may never see the real meaning of what these new teachings can bring us.

In my opinion—and space does not permit me to offer a thorough justification of it—even the harshest critics of our young "mystics" fail to see how enormous is the gap between the practice of a spiritual discipline and the religious activities of these young people. Because they—because we—do not see this gap, because we habitually underestimate the depth of real religious practice and the quality of human effort which it demands, we are blind to the positive value which this movement may possess. This value may be nothing at all like what its young proponents imagine it is; it may be infinitesimal compared to what they claim for themselves. Yet, for all that, it may be real—very small, but real. Does our way of life have even that these days?

In writing my book, *The New Religions*, I came to the conclusion that these Eastern teachings have brought a new dimension of urgency to our whole society's inability to grasp the purpose of work in the growth and transformation of man. I also tried to show that the Eastern teachings, in reviving the ideas of religious *discipline*, may bring back the sense of the gradations of religious life. For while the all-or-nothing principle of faith communicates the ever-present exigency of the search for God, the equally important principles of compassion (in Buddhism) and catholicity (in Christianity) recognize the great forces of resistance that operate upon man in this search.

Here I can list only one or two other conclusions which my study brought home to me about the future importance of this phenomenon:

—The revitalization of the idea that in a spiritual discipline what we call moral rules are really instruments for the production of certain experiences which make the seeker directly aware of the need for transcendent inner help in the governance of his life. Thus, the external *Thou Shalt* may be organically displaced by an internal understanding of the *reasons* for "sanity" and "balance" in life.

—The Eastern cosmic scheme brings back the idea of *levels* of intelligence and consciousness in the universe. And since man in this scheme is an image of the universe, a real basis is provided for us to ask: at what level of consciousness do I exist? and: at what level of consciousness *may* I exist? This then leads to the idea of inner evolution as a result of spiritual work.

These are only a few of the ways these new religions may alter our thinking about man in the universe. The point I wish to make now is one that is only implicit in my book, but which seems to need explicit formulation if we are to understand the value of our young people's new religiosity.

What I am going to suggest may sound very odd to all parties concerned, but it seems to me that the great value of this new "religiosity" is that through it our young people are able to *entertain great ideas*. Surely one aspect of our present crisis as a civilization is that the transcendent ideas which once defined our lives have grown small in our minds. They become choked and stunted by subjective opinion, interpretation and an impatience to "test" every idea by instantly applying it to solve the overwhelming external problems of human society. Thus we have converted the great ideas of our civilization into mere ideals, which is to say that we no longer know how to take the time to understand ideas before hastily acting upon them.

We no longer believe in the value of merely entertaining ideas, of living with them without expecting anything of them. I think this prevents them from becoming a real force in our lives, something that could help to shape our aims for ourselves and for society. In any event, it is obvious that the followers of the great religious paths have come to these paths with more intense an aim than most of us have, whether we are young or old.

A spiritual path thus requires a certain preparation of the mind. I do not think we have that preparation, and neither do our young people. Yet this explosion of interest in the mystical may for many be the first step in such preparation. If so, it is surely mistaken of us either to condemn it by likening it to some of the ways we ourselves have misused religious ideas or naively to extol it by putting it in a class with the great spiritual paths of mankind.

I recently saw the preliminary rushes of a film being produced in California which deals with this whole phenomenon. The makers of the film took their cameras to these groups and teachers without any pretense of judging their authenticity, and a very broad spectrum is thereby revealed: from the silence and seriousness of the young Zen Buddhists in their California monastery to the glazed eyes and dreamy smiles of naked men and women being led in meditation by a man who calls himself a Sufi master. I had previously witnessed much of this first-hand during the writing of my own book, but what made the evening so instructive was that the film-makers had also gone to India to interview some religious leaders. Sandwiched amid all that footage of gurus speaking about "oneness with God" were a few brief frames taken inside some temple of a gaunt *fakir*, his emaciated arms twisted behind him, his legs folded beneath him, his tongue stretched out and down its full length, and his wide-open eyes staring unblinkingly into the brilliant mercury lamp. He did not move a muscle, and one knew he had kept that posture for longer than one would dare imagine.

To the educated Westerner, this fakir would epitomize much that is hateful about religion: the apparent denial of the body, the violence to natural impulses, the withdrawal from life and men. Yet judge it as one may, one instantly recognized *effort*. He was on a *path*, demanding of him a scale of effort which must strike us as staggering. And we must assume that a comparable quality of effort is one way or another required by all psychospiritual disciplines, whether it be in the obedience of a Christian monk, the Herculean pondering of a *jnama-yogi*, or in the transcendent flexibility of a Sufi searching for a new consciousness in the midst of the pulls and shocks of ordinary life.

The contrast is unmistakable between the rigors of a *path* and the activity of our young people. But having sensed even a little of this contrast, we can be freer in our minds to allow them their attraction to the religions of the East, and see it, in part, as a process of opening their minds to new ideas. When we see a group of beardless youths robed in yellow, tendering alms-bowls and chanting "Hare Krishna" along Fifth Avenue, need we assume that they are either following or degrading the path of *bhakti-yoga*, a discipline that demands a lifelong struggle against all the powerful emotions that scatter our lives into a thousand pieces? May we not rather see them, some of them at any rate, as *entertaining* the idea of service as a method of psychological change? They may strike us as absurd or offensive—perhaps because we feel they are only playing at being monks. But what if most of them are only playing? How much of the sorrow of our civilization is due to the fact that *we* do not entertain ideas before acting on them—persuading, institutionalizing, making war in their name?

The phenomenon of "the new religions" therefore points to a flaw in our society of which we may have been unaware: namely, that we lack a means by which new thought can enter into our lives without inner or outer violence. We are unaware of it, because we do not believe it even to be possible. We look for ideas to come at us with proofs, arguments and, above all, with clear prescriptions for action. We seek to be persuaded, compelled or even seduced by ideas: witness our forms of art, our methods of philosophy and the manner in which we have tied scientific speculation to technology. But perhaps it is impossible for transcendent ideas—ideas that come from a more fundamental level of intelligence—to take root in this way.

The new religions, being a call to direct experience, nevertheless compel us to think in a new way about our situation in the universe; warning us against mere thought, they stir our thought. And it is very interesting how thought that has been shaken is no longer "mere" thought, how the shocked intellect is no longer the isolated intellect. I think it can be said that a religion which does not astonish the mind cannot change human life. Conversely, a mind which is insulated against shocks cannot understand the sense of religion. We have grown so accustomed to denigrating religion because of its sentimentality or its comforting fables that we are somewhat at a loss when a religion comes along which has none of these aspects.

So, while admitting the possibility that our young "mystics" are deceiving themselves, admitting that they may often confuse intense experience (whether from drugs, radical politics, sex, or something else) with psychological growth, admitting even that none of them may be able to assimilate the teachings of a few truly extraordinary spiritual masters who have come to the West—admitting all this as possibly true, the outstanding question remains whether we who may not be drawn to these new religions are necessarily more intelligent than these young people. By "intelligence" I mean: the ability to place oneself in the face of great ideas which surpass our understanding, but which demand our best thought.

RELIGION & THE OCCULT: THE RESURGENCE OF MAGIC

Magic has always been an important component of Western religion. It has also been used to describe occult learning and practices. However, although magic usually refers to evil doings, there are many magical aspects of religion that make it difficult to separate the one from the other. In the Judeo-Christian tradition, for example, it can be argued that the act of prayer is nothing more than a magical ritual aimed at bending the transcendent to one's will. Since the mysterious rituals of occultists can be similarly described, some may conclude that there is no difference between prayer and magical incantation.

However, while magic is integral to religion, it is also qualitatively different from religion as we know it. Magic has come to be associated in Western culture with what are felt to be illegitimate and sometimes evil methods for getting at supernatural forces alleged to be outside the realm of accepted religious transcendence. Perhaps central to the difference between magic and religion is the fact that magic is the attempt by man to control and use for his own purposes the mysterious forces in the universe, whereas religion is the effort to be in harmony with, or even controlled by, a transcendent reality. Underlying this difference is the distinction between the active and passive roles of the individual vis-à-vis a supernatural or transcendent force. The magician seeks to manipulate occult forces; the religious person endeavors to put his life into conformity with the will of the transcendent power.

In contemporary Western culture, the expressions of magic occur along a broad continuum extending from the scientific aspects, such as parapsychological research, to the esoteric aspects, such as astral projection. Before the emergence of the drug scene, dabblers in the occult could be described mostly as oddballs, misfits, and gullible lower-class individuals susceptible to the belief that interest in the occult is a form of intellectual pursuit of truth. In other words, until recently occultists did not receive either much esteem or much attention. Indeed, the public felt that for the most part occultists were merely harmless, albeit misguided, people. It was not until our society absorbed the effects of psychedelic drugs that it became evident that along with creating a resurgence of interest in mystical experiences, psychedelics produced a renewed desire to explore the occult—the use of psychedelic drugs by the youth culture encouraged a revival of interest in magical experiences throughout society.

Not only has interest in the occult picked up but it has spread from the marginal individuals, who traditionally have toyed with the "black arts," to the youth culture, and it is now beginning to move beyond the young. In effect, the revival of occultism has pervaded our culture to such a degree that it is not unusual to find suburban housewives, who ten years ago might have occupied their weekday afternoons with bridge, holding seances or, perhaps, Satanic rites in their living rooms.

It is believed that the current interest in the occult can be traced to the failure of contemporary religious institutions to satisfy man's natural religious impulses. It should not be surprising, then, that the occult has attracted a large proportion of bored and dissatisfied persons of all ages. The occult serves fragmented needs and has a tendency to become demonic. This aspect of the occult is particulary associated with negative drug experiences. Psychedelics can open up the dark side of man, especially to those who are susceptible to antisocial sentiments. It is precisely these individuals who, having experienced the power of evil as a result of their expanded consciousness during a drug experience, turn to witchcraft, Satanism, and similar forms of the occult.

Thus, while it may be true that occultism is multifaceted it also appears that there is a definite pattern to the expression of the occult in our society. At one level the movement attracts people with a strong commitment to occult beliefs, while at another level we are all dabblers in the occult to the extent that we are even mildly superstitious. Furthermore, there is evidence that a deep interest in the occult has penetrated mass society to a point where either consciously or unconsciously we are subject to its impact in our everyday lives.

In California in 1969 actress Sharon Tate and six others died in a brutal, ritualistic murder. Later it was revealed that the convicted murderer, Charles Manson, as well as his victims had been involved in the occult. As shocking as this case was, it was merely the most publicized example of the witchcraft, Satanism, and occultism that have been moving like a dark shadow over America. It is surely an anomaly that in a nation whose motto and heritage are "In God We Trust," there are at least ten million Americans who dabble in some form of the occult.

As the precursor of the occult, superstition is taught to most of us as children. Have you ever turned around to keep a black cat from crossing your path? Or have you ever gone out of your way to avoid walking under a ladder? If you have, you were practicing a form of witchcraft. Most superstitions that are practiced daily have their origin in witchcraft.

It was once thought that sneezing meant that the soul had temporarily left the body, and the charm "God bless you" was used to keep an evil spirit from taking over the body while it was without a soul. Knocking on wood, a common means of warding off evil, grew from the idea that wood was a symbol of all the forces of nature. When one knocked on wood he was trying to bend nature to his will. Crossing the fingers is also a custom thought to bring good luck. It grew from the crossed fingers as a representation of the cross, always a powerful symbol for warding off evil. The supposition that walking under a ladder meant bad luck grew from the belief that the devil lurked under the ladder leaning against the cross on which Christ was crucified in an attempt to snatch his soul. Although he was foiled in that attempt, he waits under ladders for other souls. The devil was thought to take the form of a black cat when he roamed the world, and black cats are also thought to be the means by which witches communicated with the spirit world. Carving initials on trees was a practice of witch children, who thought that, as a result, the couple would be magically united forever. The wedding veil was originally used to protect the bride from the evil eye of a rejected lover. Salt was considered a bond of friendship, which was broken if the salt was spilled; the bond could be reestablished by throwing a pinch of it over the left shoulder.

The use of makeup is also said to stem from witchcraft. Makeup, and especially mascara, was believed to ward off evil. Since people with eyebrows that grew close together were suspected of witchcraft, eyebrow plucking began in the Middle Ages to avoid such suspicion. Then there is the number thirteen, the wearing of charms, stepping on cracks in the sidewalks, and on and on.

Perhaps most of us performed some of these superstitious rites as children, but today children learn about the occult in a more overt way. Christmas 1971 was the season of the occult toy. Santa had something for all ages. Ouija boards, after forty years of sluggish sales, have leaped to well over two million sales in the last three years. The boards, used in communicating with the spirits, sold for only $3.95. It was even cheaper to buy the "Magic Ball Fortune Kit" or the "Genuine Vampire Kit," complete with teeth and vampire blood. Milton Bradley had several offerings: "Voice of the Mummy," an Egyptian-type magic game; "Which Witch?"; and "Barnabas Calling," a vampire game, the winner of which gets to wear fangs. In addition, there were numerous astrology games and at least one $2.50 zodiac kit for making your own zodiac medallions.

Teenagers can more than likely learn about the occult formally in school. In spite of the Supreme Court rulings regarding religion in public schools, an estimated 30 percent of the public high schools and colleges in the United States teach about the occult in courses or lecture series. Television series such as "Night Gallery," "The Sixth Sense," and "Bewitched" also are informative about the occult.

It is estimated that at least 5 million Americans plan their entire lives by the stars, while other millions consult the daily horoscope. Some 1,220 of the 1,750 daily newspapers in this country carry horoscopes. There is enough business to keep ten thousand full-time and one hundred seventy-five thousand part-time astrologers at work. An estimated 40 million Americans have turned the zodiac business into a $200-million-a-year enterprise. Currently there are several computers engaged in the casting and interpretation of horoscopes. One of these prints out a ten-thousand-word scope in minutes for twenty dollars. Another provides twenty-four-hour-a-day horoscopes to about two thousand campuses across the country. A third computer is located in Grand Central Station, putting out about five hundred horoscopes a day.

The popularity of witchcraft is also increasing. One can rent a witch to put spirit into one's parties through an agency in Cleveland. The agency will send you a good witch for between twenty-five and two hundred dollars. The witches specialize in Tarot card reading, I Ching, seances, palm reading, and fortune telling. Besides the growing number of occult shops, where you might buy anything from bat's blood to a goat's hoof and charge it on your BankAmericard, there are numerous records on the stands that deal with how to practice witchcraft. These range from "Barbara the Grey Witch," which tells the listener whether he or she is born a witch or a warlock, to "The Satanic Mass," which features Anton LaVey reading from his Satanic Bible, a book that is outselling the Holy Bible by about 100 to 1 in some areas of the country with a heavy concentration of students.

It is in the book field that the occult boom is especially evident. *Rosemary's Baby* exploded into a best seller, was made into a movie, and quickly grossed 40 million dollars. It ranks among the top fifty all-time hits in the motion-picture industry. Jeanne Dixon's book *The Gift of Prophecy* has gone through twenty-five paperback editions, selling nearly 3 million copies. The recently created Universe Book Club, a division of Doubleday, has attracted one hundred thousand members in its brief two-year history.

As one final indication of the rising popularity of the occult in the

United States, the University of California, on June 16, 1970, gave the first Bachelor of Arts degree in Magic ever conferred in this country.

While the character of occultism is generally somewhat playful, there are occultists who are serious. They are a minority, but because they tend to organize they are at the forefront of the movement. These are the people who tend to arrive at the point of commitment to occultism through more and more experience with the occult. They are also finding spiritual meaning and, perhaps because of their disenchantment with the institutional church, are moving in the direction of a religious organization that is both noninstitutional and democratic.

Marcello Truzzi, the foremost sociologist of the occult, provides some order to the field of the occult by defining the terms.[1] According to Truzzi, proto-scientific occultism is best exemplified by parapsychology; private mystical occultism by spiritualism;[2] quasi-scientific occultism by astrology;[3] shared mystical occultism by such practices as Eastern mysticism and transcendental meditation; and pragmatic occultism by magical practices and witchcraft. Although all of these categories of the occult manifest the resurgence of magic, in this section we shall limit ourselves to witchcraft, or pragmatic occultism, because it is this level of the occult movement which seems to illustrate more of the characteristics of a religious movement.

The first reading, "Straight from the Witch's Mouth" by John Fritscher, is a rambling interview between Fritscher and one of the more publicly recognized witches in the country, Anton LaVey. What he says about himself, the craft, and the cult is often revealing. The second reading is my own article, "Which Witch? Some Personal and Sociological Impressions." This article was generated from my own interviews with numerous witches, especially a benign Satanist named Herbert Sloane and a white witch named Roberta Kennedy. The final reading is the chapter entitled "The Twisted Roots," from Arthur Lyons' book *The Second Coming: Satanism in America*. In this chapter Lyons draws upon anthropological, sociological, and psychological theories to explain the revival of magic, witchcraft, and Satanism in America.

1. Marcello Truzzi, "Definitions and Dimensions of the Occult: Towards a Sociological Perspective," *Journal of Popular Culture*, 5, no. 3 (Winter 1971), 635–46. Also see his "The Occult Revival as Popular Culture: Some Random Observations on the Old and the Nouveau Witch," *The Sociological Quarterly*, 13, no. 1 (Winter 1972), 16–36.

2. For a historical treatment of both parapsychology and spiritualism see David Techter, "PSI: Past, Present, Future," *Journal of Popular Culture*, 5, no. 3 (Winter 1971), 647–54.

3. On astrology see Martin Marty, "The Occult Establishment," *Social Research*, 37, no. 2 (1970), 212–30.

STRAIGHT FROM THE
WITCH'S MOUTH

John Fritscher

*As men's prayers are a disease of the will, so are their creeds
a disease of the intellect.*
—Emerson, *Self-Reliance*

WITCH-HUNTING THESE DAYS IS A SNAP. IN FACT, NEW INQUISITORS HAVE
it easy since witches advertise. Where advertisement is lacking, ask
the manager of the local occult bookstore. If he is not a witch, he'll
know who is. Check out the backwater boutiques and the slightly-off-
campus shops with window signs reading "Occult Records." Catch
up on occult symbolism and casually confront anyone wearing mystic
insignia during a rock concert. (The median age of witches has
lowered drastically. Crones are out.) Read the classifieds of the local
college newspaper or the advertising in the local TV guides (free for
the taking at supermarkets). Clip addresses from the Wanton Ads
of the Underground Press or from overground tabloids like *The National Enquirer.*

Let your fingers do the walking through the Bell System's Yellow
Pages (pop culture's surest and handiest index): check listings for
astrologers, astrology schools, and palmists. In every instance, ask the
persons listed what they think about witchcraft. (What they're advertising is often not what they're selling. Witches advertise as
palmists because of Dis(ney)-crimination against witches. After all,
in the popular mind what does a witch do? *Witch* is too indirect a

"Straight from the Witch's Mouth." From *Popular Witchcraft*, by John
Fritscher (Bowling Green, Ohio: Bowling Green University Popular Press,
1972), pp. 89–90; 107–22. Copyright © 1972 by the Bowling Green University
Popular Press. Reprinted by permission of the publisher.

come-on. *Palmist, astrologer, numerologist* are titles specific of what the consumer expects and will get.) In any group of seven or more people, interrupt the conversation to ask, "Has anyone here any American Indian blood?" Always there will be someone. Try the same with: "Does anyone here know a witch?" Once a witch is found, ask for a referral to his or her friends in the Craft.

If all else fails, join a psychic encounter group or better yet the Psychic Club of Dayton, Ohio. For ten dollars this club, which advertises itself as the place "where witches and warlocks abound," will give you—besides what you deserve—an astro-twin pen pal, a Free Location Service for correspondence with others with the same interests, and a one year subscription to the Psychic Club Bulletin.

In the last analysis, witches, like beauty and smut, are in the eye of the beholder. What they say about themselves, though at times repetitious, is often more revealing than what we say. . . .

Anton Szandor LaVey, High Priest and
Founder of The Church of Satan;
San Francisco, California

I don't feel that raising the devil in an anthropomorphic sense is quite as feasible as theologians or metaphysicians would like to think. I have felt His presence but only as an exteriorized extension of my own potential, as an alter-ego or evolved concept that I have been able to exteriorize. With a full awareness, I can communicate with this semblance, this creature, this demon, this personification that I see in the eyes of the symbol of Satan—the goat of Mendes —as I commune with it before the altar. None of these is anything more than a mirror image of that potential I perceive in myself.

I have this awareness that the objectification is in accord with my own ego. I'm not deluding myself that I'm calling something that is disassociated or exteriorized from myself the godhead. This Force is not a controlling factor that I have no control over. The Satanic principle is that man willfully controls his destiny; if he doesn't, some other man—a lot smarter than he is—will. Satan is, therefore, an extension of one's psyche or volitional essence, so that that extension can sometimes converse and give directives through the self in a way that mere thinking of the self as a single unit cannot. In this way it *does* help to depict in an externalized way the Devil per se. The purpose is to have something of an idolatrous, objective nature to commune with. However, man has connection, contact, control. This notion of an exteriorized God-Satan is not new.

My opinion of succubi and incubi is that these are dream manifestations of man's coping with guilt as in the case of nocturnal emissions with a succubus visiting a man or of erotic dreams with an incubus visiting a woman. This whole idea of casting the blame off one's own sexual feelings onto convenient demons to satisfy the Church has certainly proved useful in millions of cases. When the priest is confronted one morning by a parishioner holding a stiffened nightshirt, a semen-encrusted nightgown, the priest can tell him about this "terrible" succubus who visited him in the night. They proceed to exorcise the demon, getting the parishioner off the sexual hook and giving the priest a little prurient fun as he plays with the details of its predication on some pretty girl in the village. This, on top of it all, leaves the girl suspect of being a witch.

Naturally the priest can keep his eyes open as to who fits the succubi descriptions that he's heard in the confessional. Of course, the concept of incubi and succubi has also been used by people who have engaged in what they would consider illicit sexual relations. More than one lady's window has been left open purposely for the incubus to enter—in the form of some desirable male. This can then be chalked up the next day to demonic possession. All these very convenient dodges have kept Christianity and its foibles alive for many hundreds of years.

The birth of a satanic child is another manifestation of the need to extend the Christ-myth of the virgin birth to an antithetical concept of a demonic birth, a Devil-child. *Rosemary's Baby* wasn't the first to use this age-old plot. The Devil's own dear son or daughter is a rather popular literary excursion. Certainly the Devil walks in the sinews and marrow of a man because he is the representation of fleshly deity. Any animal heritage, any natural predilections, any real human attributes would be seen in the personification of the Devil. Consequently the Devil would have offspring and be proud of them, antithetic as they are to Christianity. Instead of being ashamed the child was conceived in sin and baptized out of sin, the Devil revels in the lust-conception of his child. This child would be involved much more magically than one who was the byproduct of an environment that sought to negate at first opportunity the very motivating force—carnal desire—that produced him.

Religious artists' desexualizing of the birth process (Christ coming out of the bowels of Mary) has caused women to suffer childbirth pains much more than they need to because of the age-old collective unconsciousness that they must suffer this and the periodic suffering that comes every 28 days. Both these are attempts to stamp out or discredit what is in the animal world the most passionate feelings when the animal comes into heat at that time of the month. The "curse" of the menstrual cycle is a manufactured thing, manufactured by society that recognizes this period as one of great desire. Automatically, we have overemphasized its pains, tensions, turmoil, cramps. This taboo is not just Christian. Women have been placed in huts outside many villages. Every culture has thought she'd cause more jealousy and turmoil at this time because of this increase in her passions. Male animals fight more when the female is in heat. Having been a lion tamer, I know even the females are more combative at this time.

Christianity has put women at this time in more need of self-recrimination. This is the big difference between tribal customs and Christian: in the tribe, the woman is considered bleeding poison; in Christianity the woman is not only considered taboo, but she has to endure her pain as a "moral" reminder of her mortality and guilt. The primitive woman can give birth relatively painlessly and return to the fields. She goes through the physical act, but not through the moral agonies of the Christian woman. Such is the compounding of guilt. This kind of hypocrisy is my enemy number one.

I don't think young people can be blamed too much for their actions and antics. Although they coat their protests in ideological issues, I think what they resent most is not the actions of older adults, but the gross hypocrisy under which adults act. What is far worse than making war is making war and calling it peace and love and saying it's waged under the auspices of God or that it's the Christian thing to do. Onward, Christian soldiers and all that. I think that the worst thing about Christianity is its gross hypocrisy which is the most repugnant thing in the world to me. Most Christians practice a basic Satanic way of life every hour of their waking day and yet they sneer at somebody who has built a religion that is no different from what they're practicing, but is simply calling it by its right name. I call it by the name that is antithetical to that which they hypocritically pay lip service to when they're in church.

Take, for example, the roster of people executed for witchcraft in the Middle Ages. They were unjustly maligned because they were free-thinkers, beautiful girls, heretics, Jews, or people who happened to be of a different faith than was ordained. They were mercilessly tortured and exterminated without any thought of Christian charity. The basic lies and propaganda of the Christian Fathers added to the torment of the people. Yet the crime in today's streets and the mollycoddling of heinous criminals is a byproduct of latter-day Christian charity. Christian "understanding" has made our city streets unsafe. Yet helpless millions of people, simply because they were unbelievers or disbelievers, were not "understood." They were killed. It's not right that a mad dog who is really dangerous should be "understood" and those who merely dissent from Christianity should have been killed. At the Church of Satan we receive lots of damning letters from people condemning us in the most atrocious language. They attest they are good Christians; but they are full of hate. They don't know if I'm a good guy or a bad guy. They only know me by the label they've been taught: that Satanism is evil. Therefore they judge me on the same basis those people did in the thirteenth through sixteenth centuries. These very same people hardly ever get worked up over a murderer.

I think, in short, that Christ has failed in all his engagements as both savior and deity. If his doctrines were that easily misinterpreted, if his logic was that specious, let's throw it out. It has no place. It is worthless to a civilized society if it is subject to gross misinterpretation. (I'm not just protesting the "human element" in Christianity the way Christians do when something goes wrong with their system. I void the whole of the system that lends itself to such misinterpretation.) Why the hell didn't the writers mean what they said or say what they meant when they wrote that stupid book of fables, the Bible? This is the way I feel about it.

Anybody who takes up the sanctimonious cult of white light is just playing footsy with the Christian Fathers. This is why the bane of my existence are these white witches, white magicians, people who'd like to keep their foot in the safety zone of righteousness. They refuse to see the demonic in themselves, the motivations Satan's Majesty and Nature has placed inside them for their terrestrial goal. Materialism is part of Satanism, but a right kind of materialism. Everyone wants to acquire. The only thing wrong with money is it falls into the wrong hands. This makes it a curse, a disadvantage rather than an advantage. The marketplace is full of thieves. Easy wealth may be something would-be Faustian Satanists would like to get ahold of. In my experience people have come to me after I had opened doors for them. They come back wanting to know how to turn "it" off as they have more troubles than they had before. Once I offer to people what they think they want, given a week to think it over, they get cold feet. Success is a threat. Threatened by success, most people show their true colors. They show they need a god or an astrological forecast to really lay the blame on for their own inadequacy in the threatening face of imminent success.

Man needs religion, dogma, ritual that keeps him exteriorized outside of himself to waylay his guilt and inadequacy. Men will always, therefore, search for a god. We should, however, be men in search of man. The man in search of God is the masochist: he is the world's masochist. There are more than we imagine.

In the beginning I may not have intended Satanism to evolve into an elitist movement. But experience has taught me that Satanism can be a mass movement insofar as its basic pleasure-seeking premise is concerned. You build a better mousetrap, and people are going to flock to it. A pleasure principle is going to be more popular than a pleasure denying. I can't help attracting the masses. As for the people who practice a truly Satanic way of life, you can't expect the masses to transcend mere lipservice to the pleasure-seeking principle and get into the magical state of the Absolute Satanist. The Absolute Satanist is totally aware of his own abilities and limitations. On this self-knowledge he builds his character.

The Absolute Satanist is far removed from the masses who look for Satanic pleasure in the psychedelics of the headshops. We Satanists are magically a part of all this surface. I realize what my magical lessons have done, the things I've stumbled upon. We necessarily spawn our neo-Christian masses seeking their sense of soma through pills and drugs. Certainly I don't oppose this for other people who get stoned out of their minds. When they do this, the more material things there will be for me and my followers since all those people who freaked themselves out on drugs will be satisfied with their pills and will move off to colonies based on drugs. The rest of us, the Materialists, will inherit the world.

Actually, I'm very much opposed to drugs from a magical point of view, from a *control* point of view. I feel drugs are antithetical to magic. The pseudo-Satanist or pseudo-witch or self-styled mystic who predicates his success on a drug revelation is only going to succeed within his drugged peer group. His miracles go no farther than his credibility. This type of witchery is limited. This, I say, despite the fact that the druggies are no longer just a marginal group, but are a very large subculture which threatens to be the New Spirituality or the New Mysticism or the New Non-Materialism. They don't realize the whole concept of witchery is manipulation of other human beings. Druggies are not manipulative witches. To manipulate someone you've got to be able to relate to that someone. Their idea of witchery is not witchcraft so much—in the sense of witchery being manipulative magic—as witchery equalling revelation of a spiritual nature. Their superego gets developed through the use of drugs. This superego can be the earmark of a new world of drones who, through soma, would attain superegos which allow them while so controlled to think they have superiority over those really enjoying the fruits of the earth. This is why as the leader of the Satanic movement I have to examine these popular movements in the culture from a very pragmatic point of view.

The point is there will always be, among the masses, substitutes for the real thing. A planned way of life—not drugs—gets the materialist what he wants. There's nothing wrong with color TV and cars in the garage as long as the system which provides them respects law and order—a terribly overworked term. But as long as people don't bother other people, then I think this is an ideal society. I'm in favor of a policeman on every corner as long as he doesn't arrest people for thinking their own way or for doing within the privacy of their own four walls what they like to do.

We haven't been hassled too much by the law because we have so many policemen in our organization. I'm an ex-cop myself. I worked in the crime lab in San Francisco and I've maintained my contacts. They've provided for me a kind of security force. But all in all we have a very clean slate. We are very evil outlaws in theological circles, but not in civil.

How could we murder? We—unlike Christians—have a real regard for human bodies. The Satanist is the ultimate humanist. The Satanist realizes that man can be his own worst enemy and must often be protected against himself. The average man sets up situations for himself so he can be a loser. We Satanists have ancient rituals which exorcise these needs for self-abasement before they happen. We wreck Christians' tidy little dreams. When you have somebody rolling orgasmically on the floor at a revival meeting claiming an ecstasy, you tell them they're having a "forbidden" orgasm and they hate you for enlightening them. You've robbed them of their "succubus," of their freedom from guilt. They push their evilness on to us. In this sense, then, we are *very* evil.

I needn't send my child to a private school. Why should I when children are, in fact, all Satanists. She has no trouble at school. Ironically enough, the majority of our members are that often-attacked silent middle class. At least fifty percent of our members have children; the other fifty percent are not rebels, but they're not losers.

I was very liberal in my younger years. I would have been thrown into prison during the McCarthy purge had I been of any prominence. I was ultra-liberal, attending meetings of the Veterans of the Spanish Civil War, the Abraham Lincoln Brigade, the Revisionist

Movements of Israel's founding. This was all very liberal at the time. I was always for civil rights. I had Negro friends when Negro friends weren't fashionable. A man should be judged on his accomplishments, his kindness and consideration for others. A certain planned form of bigotry may be a little healthy. I mean, if a person is the worst that his race has produced, he should be prevented from using his race unless he is a credit to his race, religion, whatever it is.

Martin Luther King was killed because he was an articulate gentleman, concerned about his wife and family. He tried to do things in a mannerly way. A man like that belongs on a pedestal. But these loud baboons—and I choose the term—are nothing but rabblerousers, spewing venom. The more a person has at stake the more he watches his p's and q's. This is my test of a person's sincerity. The public is no judge. The public is not too particular in its choosing of heroes.

I voted for Wallace to act out a magical ritual. I performed it— knowing he would not win, but wishing simply to cast my runes. Wallace's advantage was he would have been helpful in the inert area between action and reaction. The pendulum is swinging. I've been misinterpreted when I've said people like Reagan and Nixon are doing a lot to help Satanism because they are causing tremendous popular reaction whereby we're getting off the hook in Vietnam.

Popular opinion is simply a reaction against the leaders who have made their stand so heinous that the protesters don't realize they're doing exactly what the masters want them to do: they're getting the masters off the hook. The masters are using the old magical technique of allowing the people to think its their idea. This explains the government's permissive attitude toward protest. The idealists of the early fifties during the McCarthy era were certainly just as against violence; but the Government posture did not lie in that direction so they had to be shut up fast. Currently the show of rebellion is, therefore, a very magical ritual.

The new emphasis will be placed on staging. Life is a game and we'll realize it's a game. Life is not "God's Will." We have to go to the point of no return before we can return. We will get to the point where anybody who is establishment oriented is suspect as being the worst kind of individual. This will happen before we return to a rather safe normality, to a sane discrimination as to who are really the contributing members of society and who are the cancerous tissue.

Satanically speaking, anarchy and chaos must ensue for awhile before a new Satanic morality can prevail. The new Satanic morality won't be very different from the old law of the jungle wherein right and wrong were judged in the truest natural sense of biting and being bitten back. Satanic morality will cause a return to intrigue, to glamour, to seductiveness, to a modicum of sexual lasciviousness; taboos will be invoked, but mostly it will be realized these things are fun.

The various Liberation Fronts are all part of the omelet from which the New Satanic Morality will emerge. Women's Liberation is really quite humorous. Supposedly women were liberated after the Industrial Revolution when they got out of the sweatshops. They're going to defeat themselves because they're not using the ammunition of their femininity to win as women. They're trying to reject their femininity which is their greatest magical weapon.

They're parodying themselves.

Speaking of parody, the historical Black Mass is a parody of a parody. The Black Mass parodies the Christian service which parodies a pagan. Every time a man and woman go to church on Sunday they are practicing a Black Mass by parodying ancient earth rituals which were practiced by their ancestors before they were *inverted* by the Christian Fathers. Our Satanic mass captures the beauty of the self and ritualizes that; the Satanic mass is no parody. It is catharsis. The Women's Libists should simply use their femininity by taking the Devil's name and using it and playing the Devil's game. They should take the stigma that cultural guilt has thrown at them and invert the values, making a virtue in their semantic reversal. This is what we have done in Satanism. What theologians have supplied in stigma, we use as virtue. We therefore have the attraction of the forbidden. This has greatly aided our success.

I know I have been rumored to have cursed Jayne Mansfield and caused her death. Jayne Mansfield was a member of the Church of Satan. I have enough material to blow sky-high all those sanctimonious Hollywood journalists. She was a priestess in the Church of Satan. I have documentation of this fact from her. There are many things I'll not say for obvious reasons. Her lover, who was a decidedly unsavory character, was the one who brought the curse upon himself. There was decidedly a curse, marked in the presence of other people. Jayne was warned constantly and periodically in no uncertain terms that she must avoid his company because great harm would befall him. It was a very sad sequence of events in which she was the victim of her own—as we mentioned earlier— inability to cope with her own success. Also the Demonic in her was crying out to be one thing and her Apparent Self demanded that she be something else. She was beaten back and forth in this inner conflict between the Apparent Self and the Demonic Self. He was blackmailing her. I have definite proof of this. She couldn't get out of his clutches. She was a bit of a masochist herself. She brought about her own demise. But it wasn't through what I had done to curse *her*. The curse was directed at *him*. And it was a very magnificent curse.

The dedication of my *Satanic Bible* to Marilyn Monroe and Tuesday Weld was, in Marilyn's case, homage to a woman who was literally victimized by her own inherent witchery potential which was there in her looks. I think a great deal of the female mystique of beauty which was personified in Marilyn's image. In the case of Tuesday Weld it's part of the magical ritual. She is my candidate of a living approximation of these other two women. Unlike them, Tuesday has the intelligence and emotional stability to withstand that which Marilyn Monroe could not. For this reason Tuesday is not in the public eye as much. Her own better judgment has cautioned her not to bite off more than she can chew.

I'd like to point out that another popular American, Ben Franklin, was a rake without question. He was a sensual dilettante. He joined up with the British Hellfire Club. Their rituals came to them from the Templars and other secret societies. We practice some of these same rituals secretly in the Church of Satan. Not only did Ben Franklin influence the activities of the Hellfire Club, his very association sheds some light on the *quality* of members of what would appear to be a blasphemous group of individuals. This proves the Devil is not only a gentleman but a cultured gentleman.

Throughout history the witch most feared is the witch most antithetical to the physical standards. In Mediterranean cultures, anyone with blue-eyes would have been the first to be named as a witch. The black woman Tituba in Salem was antithetical to New England physical standards. Anyone who is dark has an edge because of all the connotations of black arts, black magic, the dark and sinister side of human nature. Tituba probably was not only more feared but also more sought after. She was set apart physically from the rest of the people. She was the magical outsider.

The Church of Satan does not employ males as altars simply because the male is not considered to be the receptacle or passive carrier of human life. He possesses the other half of what is necessary to produce life. Woman is focal as receiver of the seed in her recumbent role as absorbing altar. A male would defeat the purpose of receptor unless he were fitted out with an artificial vagina and were physically and biologically capable of symbolizing the Earth Mother.

We do, however, accept homosexuals. We have many in the Church of Satan. They have to be well adjusted homosexuals—

and there *are* many well adjusted homosexuals who are not on the daily defensive about their sexual persuasion. Many have a great amount of life-realization. Of course, we get the cream of the crop. Since they cannot relate to the basic heterosexuality of the Church of Satan, whatever they do must be modified. If the homophile were involved in defining the dogma of our Church it would be very imbalanced for the masses of people with whom we deal. The homophile would very easily like to substitute a male for the female altar. It's a fact that a heterosexual can accept homosexuality more readily than a homosexual can accept heterosexuality. Relating to the existence of the other sex is something that MUST be in evidence. Women cannot be denied their function in our Satanic Church. Needless to add, manhating women cause us a great lack of sensual scintillation.

My book *The Complete Witch; or What to Do When Virtue Fails* is a guide for witches. It doesn't stress the drawing of pentacles on the floor. It smashes all the misconceptions that women have had, not only about witchery but about their own sexuality. I think of this book like de Beauvoir's *The Second Sex.* Even if a woman is a manhater, she can use her feminity to ruin that man. This book tells her how to do it. If she wants to enjoy men, this book will open her eyes to a few things.

Sexual fetishes we find natural. Everybody has one. These should be catered to. Sexual deviations are only negative factors when they present an obstacle to one's success. They present an obstacle when they are carried out of the ritual chamber, out of the fantasy room into the world where others will see them disapprovingly.

I must tell you something quite amusing. *Rosemary's Baby* did for us what *The Birth of a Nation* did for the Ku Klux Klan. I never realized what the film could do. I remember reading at the premiers of Griffith's *Birth of a Nation* recruiting posters for the KKK in southern cities. I chuckled because at the premiere of *Rosemary's Baby* there were posters of the Church of Satan in the lobby. Here at the San Francisco premiere there was a great deal of consternation, but the film started an influx of very worthwhile new members. Since *Rosemary* the quality of membership has gone up. Immeasurably.

Since that film with Polanski, I am constantly confronted with scripts by thick-skulled exploitation producers who want me either to be technical advisor or play the role of the Devil or the Satanic doctor in their new films. They think to one-up *Rosemary*. What they don't realize is that *Rosemary's Baby* was popularly successful because it exploded a lot of the preconceptions of Satanism: it didn't chop up the baby at the end. It threw all the crap down the drain and showed the public who was expecting the sensational the real image of the Satanist. It will remain a masterpiece.

The allegory of the Christ child in reverse is simply the birth of the new Satanic Age, 1966. The year 1966 was used in *Rosemary's Baby* because it was our Satanic Year One. The birth of the baby was the birth of Satanism. *Rosemary's Baby* stands four-square against the popular image of child sacrifice. The role that I played in the picture—the devil in the shaggy suit—was not from my point of view anything other than it should have been: man, animal, bestial, carnal nature coming forth in a ritualized way. The impregnation of Rosemary in that dream sequence was to me the very essence of the immodest, the bestial in man, impregnating the virginal world-mind with the reawakening of the animalism within oneself. This impregnation was very meaningful because it spawned literally the Church of Satan. Among all the rituals in the film, this was the big ritual in *Rosemary's Baby*.

These others who want my opinion on their scripts are simply producing more trash of the blood-sacrifice variety. In *Rosemary's Baby*, the girl who went out the window and landed on the pavement died in the pure Satanic tradition. She had made it clear—although the people who saw the film didn't realize it—that she was a loser. Everything she said pointed to it. She'd been kicked around. She'd been on the streets. She'd been on dope. She was obviously the wrong girl to be a carrier. Satan saw her lack of maternal instinct, of winning instinct, of spunk to carry this baby out into the world. She therefore sort of fell "accidentally" out the window. The end of the film shows Rosemary throw away her Catholic heritage and cherish the devil-child. The natural instinct of Satanism wins out over man-made programming.

Even though I have done the consulting for *Mephisto Waltz* for Twentieth Century Fox, that film still has the old elements of witchery. It's going to take a lot to come up with a film that's as much a blasphemy as *Rosemary's Baby*. Polanski's other film *The Fearless Vampire Killers* is like nothing else that's ever been done before in the film world. That film explodes all the puerile Christian myths about vampires. The old professor, sort of a Count Dracula, is shown to be not only the doddering old fool he really is but also the real victim at the end. The fact that all those unfortunate murders took place at Polanski's—his wife Sharon Tate and all the rest—was used by the press to highlight Polanski's interest in witchery and Satanism. The deaths had nothing to do with the films. The Polanskis were simply plagued with hippies and drug addicts. If I were to allow it, my house would be full of the sycophantic loungers. If I neglected them, they'd be paranoid. I would have been in the same position as those people at Polanski's house had I allowed it. He attracted, as people in Hollywood do, all the creeps, kooks, and crackpots. He wasn't around to stop it or was too nice to put his foot down. He, in a sense, put himself in much the same position as Jayne Mansfield.

Those people that were killed were all freaked out of their minds anyway. They were people who were only a little better than the killers. As far as their warped outlooks on life, their senses of values, it was a case of the blind destroying the blind. Sharon was probably the victim of her environment, but I can't find it in myself to whitewash these people. I know firsthand how the people at the Factory and the Daisy and these other nightclubs behave. They're quite indiscriminate as to the people they take up with.

The devil in *Rosemary's Baby* was depicted as a combination of many anthropomorphic ideals of the bestial man: the reptilian scales, the fur, claws. A combination of the animal kingdom. It was not a red union suit with a pitchfork. Nor was it Pan transmogrified by Christians into a cloven-hoofed devil. *The Cloven Hoof* title of our newsletter was chosen precisely for its eclectic image in the popular mind as one of the devil's more familiar and acceptable traits. Cloven-hoofed animals in pre-Christian times had often been considered sacred in their association with carnal desire. The pig, goat, ram—all of these creatures—are consistently associated with the devil. Hence our title.

The truest concept of Satan is not in any one animal but is in man, the evolutionary accomplishment from many animals.

The historical note that Satan has an icecold penis is a very pragmatic thing because when Satan had to service the witches who would come to him to draw from his power at the Sabbaths, he could actually remain erect either with those who stimulated him—that is the magician who portrayed Satan—or until he became expended of his sexual vigor. Naturally then, under his fur cloak or garb he had to strap on something of an artificial nature, a bull's pizzle, a dildo. In the night air, it would cool off. The witches all swore that it was cold. He would have to use something like this to maintain his position as the devil.

It is of interest to me that hippies and Hell's Angels tattoo themselves with the markings of Satanism and other symbols of aggression. Tattooing is an ancient and obscure art. One of the few books on it is called *Pierced Hearts and True Love* by Ebensten. There's also George Burchett's *Memoirs of the Tattooist*. Certainly much needs to be said of the relation of Satanism and witchery to tattooing. We have members that were tattooed long before the Hell's Angels made it fashionable. One man has the Goat of Bathona, the Satanic Goat, tattooed across his back. Beautifully done. The devil-headed eagle is on his chest. Then on each thigh he has the figure of Seth. He's quite spectacular. He has a shaven head and the build of a professional wrestler. He is extremely formidable when he is in ceremony wearing only a black pair of trunks with a very small mask across his eyes. His are very symmetrically contrived attempts at using tattoos for ritualistic purposes.

Witchcraft has a lot of show business in it. Religious ritual after all was the first theater. For this reason, I think, *Dark Shadows* and *Bewitched* are fine. White witches think these TV shows are terrible because they play the witch as a pretty girl who can snap her fingers and get things done. They try to impress the world that a *wicca* is not up to that sort of thing. They try to play that they're an intellectually justified "Old Religion." The popular image of the witch is a girl who can get things done in apparently supernatural ways. Like *I Dream of Jeannie*. Why not take advantage of the glamorized witch? If this has been the very element that has brought witchcraft out of a stigmatized, persecuted stereotype, then why put it down? It is the glamorization of witchcraft that gives the erstwhile white witches the free air in which to breathe. Why knock it?

This gets me to Gerald Gardiner, whom I judge a silly man who was probably very intent on what he was doing; he had to open a restaurant and get it filled with customers. He took over a not too successful teashop and turned it into a museum. He had to say he was a research scholar. He got the term *white witch* from a coinage in *Witchcraft's Power in the World Today*. Gardiner used the term because witchery was illegal in England at the time. To avoid persecution he opened his museum under the guise of research. He stated he wasn't a witch until the repeal of the laws in 1953. Then he made it very clear he was a white witch. That's like saying, "Well, I'm a good witch. The others are bad witches. So don't persecute me." Gardiner did what he had to do, but I don't think he was any more of an authority on the true meaning of witchcraft than Montague Summers. I think that he simply followed Summers' crappy rituals of circles and "Elohim" and "Adonai." They used the name of Jesus and crossed themselves.

I have broken the barrier. I have made it a little bit fashionable to be a black magician. A lot of them, therefore, are trying to say now that their horned god is not a Devil. It is just a horned god. Well, let me tell you, until five or six years ago they wouldn't even admit to a horned god. Suddenly they like to intimate that perhaps they have made pacts with the Devil. For many years the

Old Religionists used Albertus Magnus, the Sixth and Seventh Books of Moses, The Book of Ceremonial Magic, crossing themselves as they turned the pages, denying theirs was a Christian-based faith. Why in the hell did they use all these accoutrements? White witches are no more than a byproduct of Christianity, or they wouldn't have to call themselves white witches in the first place. I don't think white witches have the courage of their convictions.

I have said that Aleister Crowley had his tongue jammed firmly in his cheek. I think Crowley was a pragmatist. He was also a drug addict. The demons he conjured were the products of a benumbed mind. Basically he was a sweet, kind man who was trying to emancipate himself from the throes of a very strict upbringing. He can't be blamed for anything he did from a psychoanalytical point of view. He wasn't really that wicked of a man. He had to work overtime. All the arbitrary numbers, dogma, and so on of his magical curriculum were constructs he invented to answer the needs of his students. Crowley's greatest wisdom was in his *Book of Life*. The particular page can be paraphrased: "My disciples came to me, and they asked, Oh Master, give us your secret." He put them off. They insisted. He said it would cost them ten thousand pounds. They paid, and he gave them his words: "A sucker is born every minute." This says more for Crowley than all his other work. His judgement of the popular follower was accurate; most of the public wants gibberish and nonsense. He alluded to this in his numbering of his *Libers* which are not immense volumes but just a few bound sheets of paper. He's saying the real wisdom is about ten lines long.

Like Crowley, Gerald Gardiner probably knew a good thing when he saw it and got something going that turned out to be more sanctimonious than it should be. Ray Buckland began the same way. Now he admits to once being part of the more mundane rather than the complete esoteric he was made out to be. Ray Buckland certainly knows a great deal about the occult. He has a good synthesis of the Arts. But sanctimony still comes through. His famous chapter on black magic threatens that if a curse is not performed properly it will return to the sender. He defines things like good and bad, white and black magic for those who—as I say in my *Satanic Bible*—are frightened by shadows. I maintain that good like evil is only in the eyes of the beholder. Ray Buckland has guts, though, to sit in his Long Island home conducting his rituals and not caring what the neighbors think.

I don't know whether Sybil Leek is as big a fool as she sometimes seems, or whether she's laughing up her sleeve. Sybil is a good business woman. I don't want to judge her—if she is a good business woman she knows on which side her bread is buttered! My only complaint with Sybil—and I do know her personally—is she has done nothing to dispel all the crap about black and white witches. If she's after the little old ladies in tennis shoes, fine. But she is a dispenser of misinformation.

Alex Sanders has become more public in proclaiming himself the King of the Witches. He is a dispenser of misinformation too. He's not too bad; in the stifling climate of England he's a forward man among a backward people. He's got a big load. For this I admire him. He's great enough to claim himself King. I don't put much credence in astrology—it's a case of the tail wagging the dog. A competent sorcerer, however, should know his astrology because it is a motivating factor for many people. Sydney Omarr, the popular syndicated astrologer, is basically a level-headed guy who sees through a lot of the fraud.

I'll be the first to give Sybil Leek and Louise Huebner and all these people their due. They don't say, "We witches don't want publicity." That takes moxie in a sanctimonious society. They're not like these damn cocktail party witches who can't defend their self-styled reputations when called to do it. These people give me a pain. It's part of being a witch, the ego gratification of being a witch, to want to talk about it in detail in public.

WHICH WITCH? SOME PERSONAL & SOCIOLOGICAL IMPRESSIONS

Edward F. Heenan

I HAD NEVER MET A "BLACK WITCH" WHO BELIEVED IN SATHANUS. To be sure I had read and seen pictures of Anton LaVey in articles about Satanism in *Time* magazine and *McCalls*. I sensed futility, a carnival atmosphere, and entrepreneurship in those articles—the former circus employee's somewhat vaudevillian attempt to play at the game of evil for his own profit. Nevertheless, Anton LaVey was at least a credible name for someone who publically claimed to be in league with the devil. But Herbert Sloane? That was hardly a name that conjured up visions of the devil. I recalled Hannah Arendt's book on the banality of evil, her study of Adolph Eichman. After some time thinking about such banalities, it still seemed to me that the devil would be more apt to choose a man named Adolph to do his will than a man called Herb, no matter how banal the endeavor.

Beyond the poor choice of his name, there was another inconsistency to the scene. I was speeding across the flat and fertile surface of Ohio to meet Dr. Sloane at his home in a city that is more often referred to as "Holy Toledo." Could anything uncommonly evil be nurtured in Toledo, the tired old industrial city in the heartland of the United States? Certainly Satan's recruitment practices would be more successful if they were directed toward America's Babylon and Nineveh, New York and California. After all, everything loose in the United States heads either to the East or to the West coast.

Other than these relatively minor oversights on the part of Satan —the fact that he is not perfect has been clearly documented—the scene was right. I was armed with my eastern Irish-Catholic upbringing, which lent a distorted air of credibility to Satan. However, this mind-set was nicely balanced by a Ph.D. in the scientific discipline of sociology—a science that specializes in debunking such superstition and relegates the person of Satan not to the regions of Hell but to the internal lattices of misfiring social structures. When I began my trip to Toledo the lugs of my mind machine were prepared to grind out sociological concepts. I was going on a debunking outing.

Yet somewhere in my past my ancestors undoubtedly really believed in leprechauns and fairies. I could not overcome the thought that there was at least a chance that the personality and career of Satan, recorded throughout human history, was just as real as those intangibles we call social structures. If there were good little fairies, why not big bad demons also? Could it be that we have even depersonalized evil and laid the blame on amorphous and ill-formed structures? But that was coming dangerously close to engaging in shortcut thinking, again a result of my upbringing. I hastily retreated to the comfort of the scientific method. It is a method that is so difficult and meticulous that when it is properly followed, one is convinced that the difficulty of the process must yield its reward in the form of truth. Yes, for the moment, that was the way to discover truth—not shortcut thinking.

My reason was well trained, but my emotions were being exploited by the omen of heavy, dark clouds overhead (Hemingway had used them to symbolize impending disaster) and my patience was being tested by Dr. Sloane's directions. Since he had just moved to the East side, he had instructed me to come to 87 Ridge Park Village. He further instructed me to ask for Ridge Park Village at any gas station on the East side if I got lost. Since he claimed that it was a new development, he felt that everyone knew where it was. The directions were meager and I did get lost.

After about a half-hour of riding around the East side of Toledo, I began to regain confidence in my ability to deal with the empirical world. First, I was right about those clouds—the first drops of rain were beginning to fall; and second, Dr. Sloane was wrong—nobody knew exactly where Ridge Park Village was. I was already late for my eight o'clock appointment with the doctor when I was further frustrated by having to wait for a fifty-car train to pass only two blocks away from what someone assured me was Ridge Park Village. All of the cars were loaded with coal (somewhat appropriately) shipped from the depths of Southern Ohio or West Virginia and headed for the furnaces of Detroit—fuel for the structures of a complex society. I began to hope that the directions would be wrong again and I could go home, having at least tried.

The sign said Ridge Park Village, but Dr. Sloane's "new development" did not turn out to be the modern apartment complex with sliding glass doors, bricked patios, and gaslights that I had pictured, using its name as my only clue. It was in fact a World-War-II-vintage housing project—a sprawling complex of single-unit two-story dwellings that proved to be a little more successful in preserving dignity than the abortive uplifting attempt of the high-rise. But not even sociologists knew that from the beginning.

As I slowly drove through the narrow streets of the complex from one speed bump to the next looking for number 87, I noticed that a majority of the faces were black or brown. This did not surprise me at all: I knew the statistics of poverty and housing. What did surprise me was the realization that perhaps the title "black witch" that was applied to Herbert Sloane did not apply at all to the type of magic he engaged in but rather to his skin color.

When I pulled into the parking area across from number 87, I caught a glimpse of a young white man with long black hair and a full beard looking out of the kitchen door. Well, another theory destroyed by a simple empirical fact; my black witch was white. That conclusion was correct, but based on false evidence. The young man was Terry, a witch in his middle twenties who designed the displays in one of Toledo's more attractive department stores. The old man behind him, who greeted me warmly, was Dr. Herbert Sloane.

WHITE SATANISM

Dr. Sloane is a portly man only a few months away from his sixty-seventh birthday. His kind, grandfatherly image is not even destroyed when one realizes that he is in his basic Satanic uniform. The uniform consists of black shoes, pants, and tie, with a white shirt and white socks. It is highlighted by a satanic tie-pin and matching cuff-links. His hair is white and augmented by a white Hitler-type mustache and a short, neatly trimmed beard. Yet even this extra hair and his long, sharpened fingernails did not make him look particularly austere. Rather his grooming indicated that he was adept at his lifetime trade. Herbert Sloane is a retired barber.

I was invited to sit in the blue, cinderblock living room while Herb prepared us each a cup of coffee. Still cautious, I had mine without cream and sugar. While I waited I glanced about the room. It was small and dark, with a sofa, coffee table, one easy chair, bookcase, and office desk—a modest room that befitted the income of a recently retired barber. The only indications of this man's avocation were a plastic orange pumpkin on his desk, a clock on the wall shaped like a black cat whose eyes moved from left to right as its tail swung as a pendulum, a walking stick with a red Satanic head for a grip, an icon made with a golden-horned Satan's head in front of a black backdrop, and in the center of the sofa, propped on a pillow, an enchanted doll whose name was A.B. The doll was clothed neatly in a dress but had no distinguishable facial features. There was something inexpensive, theatrical, and slightly ludicrous about these toys. They certainly fell far short of instilling fear, mystery, or horror.

When Herb returned our conversation began. He first explained that there was nothing secretive about his coven and that he would answer any question if he could. He went on to express the hope that I could use the material in a book. Opening his bookcase, he showed me eight recent books that had mentioned his coven. The pages were clipped to make it easy for me to find the appropriate passages.[1] The intention of the interview having been made clear, he spent several hours giving me a history of his life as a servant of Sathanus. In the course of the interview I became comfortable enough to consume several cups of coffee, now with cream and sugar.

Herbert Sloane was born on a farm in North Central Ohio. It was on that farm that he first realized that he was a witch. At the age of three he was walking in the woods near his home when he saw a vision of Sathanus on a charred tree stump. It was this vision, which he finds difficult to describe, that gave direction to his whole life. From that moment he felt a unique spiritual bond between himself and Sathanus. Throughout most of his young life Herb was convinced that he was alone in his union with Sathanus. He worshipped privately as a young man and began the tedious process of reading all that he could on witchcraft and Satan.

For most of his adult life he remained a witch in solitude. He did, however, augment his knowledge of occult phenomena by studying hypnosis and fortune telling. Also, he received his doctorate in

1. For the most comprehensive interview with Dr. Sloane, see Brad Steiger, *Sex and Satanism* (New York: Ace Books, 1969).

cardology from a now defunct occult school in Ohio. In 1948, having realized that others also believed in witchcraft, he founded Our Lady of Endor Coven—The Ophitic Gnostic Cultus of Baal Sathanus in Toledo. It was at this stage in his life that he began to formulate and articulate the beliefs and rituals that now constitute his brand of Satanism.

Although the composition of Our Lady of Endor Coven has changed over the years, its size has remained consistently small. At the present time there are seven members, who range in age from twenty-two to forty-three. Terry is a decorator, another member is a barmaid, a third is a housewife, a fourth, also a woman, trims poodles, the fifth is a social worker for the Welfare department. The final two members are A.B., the enchanted doll, and a former nurse, who is now in the spirit world. Her picture is displayed on Herb's desk, and his eyes become misty when he talks of her slow death of cancer only a year ago. He enjoyed a deep relationship with this woman over a number of years and still grieves over her loss.

Herb explained that the coven could be larger (as many as thirteen members) but that he personally screens out the many young people he feels have turned to witchcraft for escapist reasons.

The seven members must meet fifteen times a year at the place where Herb resides. Thirteen of these meetings are on the night of the full moon (Sabbat), one is on April 30 (Esbat), and one is on Hallowe'en (Sathanusmass). On these occasions they celebrate their liturgy. Each of these occasions is a sacred one in the coven. It begins promptly at nine o'clock. Herb does not tolerate tardiness, and there are no excused absences. Like worshipers in Christian churches (which Herb respects), members are expected to dress in their Sabbat best out of respect for Sathanus. Jeans, slacks, pants suits, and the like are considered inappropriate for a Sabbat liturgy. Herb himself is dressed in his usual uniform, with the addition of a black cape and plastic horns on his head.

The liturgy begins with the call, the ringing of a small bell. It is followed by Herb's invocation to Sathanus to hear the prayers of the members of the coven. Next, Herb and the entire coven recite their creed in unison:[2]

2. The prayers quoted in the text are from the liturgy adopted by Our Lady of Endor Coven, The Ophitic Gnostic Cultus of Baal Sathanus in the 108,124th moon, calculating according to the Grecian Mundane Era. The Grecian Mundane Era began in 5598 B.C. These prayers are quoted with the permission of Dr. Herbert Sloane.

I believe in an Infinite Intelligence incomprehensible to all finite beings. I believe in Baal Sathanus as my savior by virtue of the Ophitic Gnosis booned by Him to Our Blessed Mother Eve in the Garden of Eden. I believe in Eve as our mundane Mother. The Blessed succubus Lilith as our spiritual Mother. I believe in Asmodeus and all the Powers and Principalities of the Celestial Realms of Baal Sathanus. I believe in the communion of the succubus and the incubus. I believe in the Gnosis of the Ophitic Gnostic Cultus Sathanus, in Magick, and in the final release of the souls of all faithful Witches from the powers of the disdained demiurge unto a life everlasting in Orcus. All this through the Power and the Goodness, the Guidance and the Wisdom of Our Baal Sathanus ———worlds without end.

Mena——Mena——Mena——Mena

After the creed Herb reads the first reading to the coven. This reading can be chosen from any source, but it usually relates to the sermon that Herb will deliver at a later point in the service. Following the first reading Herb reads the announcements that inform members of the coven of upcoming events pertinent to them. Next in the order of the service is the prayer of supplication, again delivered by Herb:

Salutations, O Baal Sathanus, who art in Orcus, we witches of this Coven do Hallow Thy name. Let ever Thy Powers and Thy Principalities come that Thy will may be made manifest among Thy faithful witches in this biosphere even as it is in Orcus. Give us this moon the guidance of Asmodeus in our vocations. Salutations, Mother Lilith, help us in our enchantments. Baal Sathanus inspire our souls to demonstrate gratitude as the highest of Thy directives, and allow us not to fall into demiurgic paths, but rather keep us ever under the Mystic Shadow of Thy Trident. Hail Blessed Mother Eve, full of wisdom. Blessed art Thou amongst Witches and Blessed is the fruit of Thy womb Cain. Hallow Mother Eve, Receiver of the Gnosis, Most Precious Mother Eve, Grandmother of Enoch, petition for us now and at the hour of our disincarnations. So be it now and forevermore worlds without end.

Mena——Mena——Mena——Mena

This prayer is followed by prayers for the benefactors of the coven and for the faithful departed of the coven. Next follows the communion rite. In this rite a chalice filled with either wine or grape juice is passed counterclockwise among the members of the coven and finally consumed by Herb himself. After communion, Herb gives the second reading and begins what is usually the longest part of the liturgy, his sermon. The sermon ends with a benediction, which concludes the service. It is followed by a social hour.

Since the liturgy was quite tame and respectable, I naturally assumed that "social hour" must be a euphemism for "orgy." To my surprise, the social hour of this Satanic coven involves no more than coffee, tea, cookies, and conversation. It was like any church social.

The belief system of Herbert Sloane is difficult to summarize. It is obvious that many of the prayers used in his liturgy are simple inversions of traditional Christian prayers. His creed is structurally similar to the Nicene creed. His prayer of supplication contains elements of both the Lord's Prayer and the Hail Mary. However, nowhere is this lack of theological imagination more evident than in the retirement prayer of Our Lady of Endor Coven:

> Now I lay me down to sleep, I pray Baal Sathanus my
> soul to keep, if I should disincarnate ere I wake, I pray
> Baal Sathanus my soul to take.
> Mena——Mena——Mena——Mena

Yet in spite of the parallels with Christianity there is one major theological difference between Herb's theology and Christian theology. Sloane is a libertine gnostic. As such, he believes that there is a god beyond the god of creation. This god is the highest of the gods and even the creator of the world is a demiurge in relation to him. This god is Baal Sathanus, who made his existence known to humans through Eve in the Garden of Eden. Aside from this major difference in theology, Herb's dogma and ritual are convoluted versions of Christian dogma and ritual.

Perhaps more revealing than what Herb believes is what he does not believe. First, Herb believes in spontaneous creation rather than evolution. Undoubtedly this rejection of evolution is dictated by the importance of the story of creation in the development of his theology. As a result, Herbert Sloane has become a unique type of biblical literalist. He also is antimaterialistic. In fact, he gave up his membership in Anton LaVey's Church of Satan because he felt that this group of Satanists was too greatly concerned with mundane things. He does not believe in the use of drugs, alcohol, or sex in his brand of Satanism. He feels that anything that could prevent Sathanus from communicating with the members of the coven must be prohibited. He even goes so far as to rule out the possibility of a homosexual being a member of the Endor coven. Finally, unlike many witches, Herb does not believe in reincarnation. He views human life as the lowest plateau of the spiritual quest. At his death a human being simply moves to a more nearly perfect dimension of reality. He continues to move to higher dimensions, and there is no return to this life in any form.

Herb does believe in magic. He defines it as the ability to affect events in conformity with his will. In spite of this belief, he claims that he is not proficient in the use of magic. Also, in spite of his Satanism he has only once attempted to use magic for the purpose of harming another individual. In most cases he has only attempted to use magic to help insomniacs sleep or to help students pass exams.

He also believes in tolerance and is, in fact, quite tolerant of other religions. He is less tolerant of those who would violate the rules of his coven and has excommunicated one member for absenteeism. There was also a time when Herb did not consider other covens to be legitimate members of the witchcult. However, in the last ten years he has mellowed a bit and is now more ecumenical. Nevertheless, he still refers to other witches as his "separated brethren."

In summary, Herbert Sloane presented a curious mixture of Satanism, Puritanism, and authoritarianism. Because of the primary place he gives to Sathanus in his belief system he is rightly called a Satanist—although a benign one. Because of his rigid moral and ethical beliefs and practices he resembles one who subscribes to the puritan ethic of some of the more traditional and conservative Christian churches. Finally, his style of leadership in organizing and controlling his coven is more characteristic of authoritarian than of charismatic leaders.

In the end I left Herbert Sloane with my own internal conflict between myth and science unresolved. Herbert simply did not fit the simplistic categories. He was not a fair test of the depth of the tension. I did, however, learn to appreciate the charm, kindness, and sincerity of one Satanist.

THE NOUVEAU WITCH

Before I left Herbert Sloane he gave me a list of witches from his correspondence file. One of those on the list whom I later interviewed was Roberta Kennedy of Dayton, Ohio.

Mrs. Kennedy is a "nouveau witch" and the founder of the Rainbow Coven in Dayton. Her coven is less than a year old; in fact she founded it before she was officially designated a witch. A few months after she founded her coven she traveled to Canada, where she was officially initiated into the craft. At any rate, both her directions and living accommodations were an improvement on Herbert Sloane's.

Mrs. Kennedy is a mother and a homemaker in her mid-thirties. She lives in a quiet suburb of Dayton. Since her husband's job necessitates it, she has lived for short periods of time in different parts of the world. Roberta herself is a nurse and is currently working in the maternity ward of a local hospital.

Mrs. Kennedy arrived at witchcraft after a long interest in both religion and the occult. She has been a member of several different Christian denominations throughout the years. She also has a certificate in graphology, which she earned through a correspondence course while in Panama, and like Herbert Sloane she is a former member of the Church of Satan. Unlike Sloane, Mrs. Kennedy left the Church of Satan because she felt that some of its members were over-enthusiastic about the use of harmful aspects of magic.

Her home gave evidence of her occult interests. The living room contained innumerable candles and several containers of burning incense as well as three or four occult paintings. Upstairs there was a room set aside for the performance of the ritual of Wicca. This room contained an altar, on which were displayed most of the paraphernalia found in occult shops, from chalice to flagella.

The Rainbow Coven is composed of five persons, four of whom are women and the fifth a bisexual male. They meet regularly at the Kennedy home for instruction, discussion, and the performance of the ritual. The ritual is done by the book (the Book of Shadows) since the knowledge of witchcraft in the coven does not extend much beyond the popular literature of the past five years. Since the members are feeling their way along, it is also appropriate that many of the rituals are performed "skyclad."

The Rainbow Coven is relatively democratic in its organization, and in the course of its short history the members have enunciated a statement of the coven's beliefs and purposes:

THIS IS THE RAINBOW COVEN

We believe that an ideal philosophy of life, as evidenced by witchcraft, enables one to adjust to one's environment and helps one to find a harmonious existence—knowing oneself and the universe, as well as respecting the balance between the forces of nature and man. This philosophy should be sufficiently flexible to permit growth for all. We acknowledge the existence of a force, or a god, that is best illustrated by two deities: a Goddess with her consort the Horned God. This force is omnipresent, but neither omniscient nor omnipotent. Witchcraft, despite its trappings, is just another way of life; a religion with the same purpose as other religions. We believe that there is much wisdom inherent in mother nature, and that in contrast to fluctuating instabilities of society, she has rhythms and cycles which are constant and dependable. We practice rituals and ceremonies to stay in tune with these natural laws. We believe in evolution and reincarnation, and that our purpose in life is to learn as much as we can so that we can all exist at maximum potential. We believe in magic and miracle as part of nature, we do not find it necessary to totally abandon all of the knowledge which our technology has supplied us.

We believe that there are very few absolutes in life and that most things can be labelled "good" or "bad" only dependent upon the circumstances in which they are found. We believe that mankind is not inherently sinful, that we can create our own heaven here on earth, and that karma is not punishment for misdeeds but an opportunity to learn and to add to previous experience. We believe in freedom controlled by responsibility and accompanied by the conformity which is necessary for group interaction. We believe in population control and favor the current growth of the ecology movement. Since some have a tendency to give lip service to things which they really do not believe, we feel that a person's faith and those things he considers sacred will best be displayed by his behavior and actions and not by the words which he speaks. We believe that honesty is the best policy, but that blunt truth should not be used to hurt others. We believe in generosity controlled by rational self-interest. We believe that sex is a sacramental union representing the love and commitment of two people for each other, and is just as sacred for the homosexual as it is for the heterosexual.

We believe in nudity as the typification of equality and as the symbolic casting off of the hypocritical restraints of the world; therefore, anyone who has such shame for his body that he is unable to disrobe before his brothers and sisters of the Wicca, is not truly free. We use and encourage experience with telepathy, precognition, hypnosis, graphology, astrology, psychometry, dowsing, psychokinesis, clairvoyance, mediumship, and all esoteric areas of the occult sciences that will further our personal development. We believe that aspirin, caffeine, nicotine, and alcohol are all drugs, and all of us who use them have no right to condemn those who have chosen different drugs to alter the state of their bodies. We do, however, condemn the abuse of drugs. We believe that there is much wisdom inherent in the Indian prayer: "Great Spirit, grant that I may not criticize my neighbor until I have walked a mile in his moccasins"; and in the serenity prayer "Grant me the serenity to accept the things I cannot change, courage to change the things I can, and wisdom to know the difference"; and in the Craft precept "If you harm none, do as you wish." [3]

This statement is in dramatic contrast to the beliefs of Herbert Sloane and the Endor Coven. First of all, each of the covens is stamped with the sexuality of its founder. There is little doubt that the Sathanus that is worshipped in the Endor Coven is a male. In contrast, the god of the Rainbow Coven is a "Goddess with her consort the Horned God." Beyond that, however, the Rainbow Coven is much more interested in maximum potential, personality growth, and group interaction. All of these interests are alien to Herbert and

3. The statement *This is the Rainbow Coven* is quoted in its entirety, and with the permission of Mrs. Roberta Ann Kennedy.

his coven. In addition, Mrs. Kennedy sees a correlation between the revival of witchcraft and the Women's Liberation Movement. She sees the witch's coven as one of the few places in society in which a woman can enjoy equality.

Aside from these broad differences of philosophy and perspective, there are a number of specific issues on which the two witches and their covens would disagree. Mrs. Kennedy believes in evolution and reincarnation, while Dr. Sloane does not. She believes in population control and the ecology movement, while Dr. Sloane has nothing to say regarding either of these contemporary movements. She adopts a liberal posture in regard to homosexuality, while his is more conservative. She does not object to nudity, alcohol, or drugs as part of her cult, while he would reject each of these as peripheral to his religion. Finally, Mrs. Kennedy endorses "all esoteric areas of the occult sciences," while Herbert Sloane prefers not even to use the term "occult" in describing his type of witchcraft.

In summary, if the words that describe Dr. Herbert Sloane's witchcraft are *Satanism, puritanism,* and *authoritarianism,* the contrasting descriptions of Mrs. Kennedy's witchcraft are *occultism, libertinism,* and *egalitarianism.*

CONCLUSIONS

Although Herbert Sloane and Roberta Kennedy are only two examples of witches, they nevertheless represent two radically different perspectives in contemporary witchcraft. In knowledge of their craft, for example, Herbert Sloane completely overshadows Roberta Kennedy. Dr. Sloane has spent years learning and integrating every aspect of the tradition of witchcraft. He is a virtual compendium of knowledge about the subject. In contrast, Mrs. Kennedy has a limited knowledge of witchcraft. Indeed, her knowledge barely goes back to books written within the past ten years. In essence, she is not familiar with witchcraft as a holistic tradition because she lacks an accurate knowledge of the history of her beliefs.

Without a sense of the history of witchcraft, Mrs. Kennedy appears unable to formulate a system of ultimate beliefs. By contrast, Dr. Sloane possesses a definite ideology or system of beliefs that places Sathanus in a primary position. Mrs. Kennedy, however, is a relativist insofar as that she does not believe in absolutes in witchcraft. To the extent that Dr. Sloane is doctrinal, Mrs. Kennedy is eclectic in belief. This is particularly evidenced by the differences in the bases for action in each of the covens. In Dr. Sloane's coven belief forms the basis for action, while in Mrs. Kennedy's coven the members do not adhere to a codified system of beliefs. Instead, Mrs. Kennedy's coven is tuned into all beliefs.

The indiscriminate belief system of the Rainbow Coven leads to another significant difference between the two perspectives in witchcraft—namely, the occult payoff. Mrs. Kennedy's coven is geared to experiencing as many different kinds of occult events as is humanly possible. In some respects, the purpose of the coven is to afford its members an opportunity to participate in the titillating activities that are forbidden by the straight world. Dr. Sloane's coven is, for the most part, unconcerned with achieving experiences of this kind.

This lack of concern with maximizing occult experiences is reflected in another difference between the two types of witchcraft. Dr. Sloane's witchcraft can be characterized as nonritualistic and, above all, austere. Mrs. Kennedy's witchcraft is deeply involved in elaborate rituals of all types. Moreover, Dr. Sloane's coven meets only fifteen times a year, while Mrs. Kennedy's coven meets about once a week. Therefore, not only do the covens practice different rituals but they have different needs for ritual. Clearly, Mrs. Kennedy's coven is dependent upon repeated performances of their rituals, while Dr. Sloane's coven is cohesive without much ritual. This is evidenced by Dr. Sloane's belief that a particular deceased person is still an active member of the coven.

Although it may be said that Dr. Sloane's and Mrs. Kennedy's covens represent radically different forms of witchcraft, they do share one common aspect. Both have a similar effect on their members. In particular, belonging to a coven allows otherwise powerless and marginal individuals to acquire a modicum of power over, as well as a sense of community with, other individuals. This is especially true for the leaders of the covens, but it is equally applicable to the rank-and-file members. The latter, at least, are able to indulge in the belief that as witches they possess supernatural powers that may be used to control the destinies of others.

In summary, there are several factors that are useful in examining the differences in witchcraft. They include knowledge about witchcraft, dogma or beliefs, the occult payoff, occult ritual, and the personal rewards achieved by belonging to a coven. These factors may be used to analyze any witchcraft or occult movement and may be especially useful in describing the future of witchcraft. Furthermore, it would appear that at a point in the not-too-distant past a reformation in witchcraft occurred. With the rise of interest in the occult, traditionalists, such as Dr. Sloane, have quickly seen a chipping away at their structure and a blossoming (at least in numbers) of new witches. These new witches seem to be the wave of the future in witchcraft.

THE TWISTED ROOTS

Arthur Lyons

*Man is still in his childhood; for he cannot respect an ideal
which is not imposed on him against his will, nor can he find
satisfaction in a good created by his own action. He is afraid
of a universe that leaves him alone. Freedom appals him.*
—George Santayana, *Reason in Religion*

MANY THEORIES HAVE BEEN PUT FORTH BY SOCIAL SCIENTISTS IN RECENT
years to explain the occurrence of witchcraft and magic in society.
Witches, devils, and hobgoblins are psychological projections, these
people say, created for the purpose of putting into concrete, tangible
form those anxieties rising out of the normal patterns of living.

Anthropologists have overwhelmingly taken the functional approach to the subject, scanning cultures to determine what particular functions a belief in witchcraft might perform for the society
as a whole. Clyde Kluckhohn, in his classic study of Navajo witchcraft, comes to the conclusion that witch-beliefs serve as an outlet for
repressed hostility. E. E. Evans-Pritchard, in his study of the Azande,
has stated that witchcraft is functional in that society in that it explains away unfortunate events. Most of these investigations have
gone on the assumption that witchcraft is indicative of the amount
of latent conflict in the culture and of the degree of repression pre-
venting these conflicts from being vented through normal social
channels. A. I. Richards has noted the growth of witch accusations
in certain East African tribes and has offered that this is a direct
outgrowth of the social ruptures caused by the clash of values between

African and European cultures in competition there. Still others have tried to relate the conflict to the battle of the sexes. Where sexual antagonism is great, they say, and males are in the ascendant position of power within the system, those accused are most likely to be women.

Some sociologists, rather than treating magic and witchcraft as release valves for accumulated tensions, have tried to link them to the entire social structure. Witchcraft is said by many following this approach to be generated most frequently in those societies which are individualistically inclined, in which the established lines of authority are weak and unclear. According to this line of reasoning, in the absence of social institutions demanding a high degree of cooperation or obedience, feelings of isolation are fostered within the individual. In such a case, the individual depends directly upon the supernatural realm to supply him with meaning for his social actions, and he thus bypasses secular institutions, which in most cultures are the normal sources of authority.

Such studies are valuable and in many cases correspond closely to truth. It is obvious that in many cultures, scapegoating serves as a means of alleviating social conflicts and plays a major role in the fostering of witch-beliefs. Throughout history, those most often accused of being in league with the powers of Hell have been those unfortunate individuals who were somehow different than the herd, who were not quite able to conform to the current modes of behavior. By fixing blame on an enemy, real or imaginary, an accuser is able to scapegoat his own misfortunes unto another, thus skirt uncomfortable feelings of failure and self-doubt. In Europe and America, those accused by their neighbors of Devil-worship were most often the old, the eccentric, the licentious, and the rebellious—in other words, all those who would be the most likely targets for repressed hatred and jealousy.

But these studies, as legitimate as they may be, cover a different area of the subject than I wish to deal with here. The psychological analyses that have been made have dealt mainly with the psychology of the belief *in* witches, rather than the beliefs *of* witches. They have tried to explain witchcraft from the outside in, but have neglected the forces motivating the witches themselves. Dealing as they do with accusations rather than with the accused, they have often treated witchcraft phenomena not as fact, but as fiction. It is true that in most cases accusations have outnumbered actual instances of practice, for reasons that scholars of the subject are eager to bring out. But it would be folly to deny the possible reality of such practices on the evidence of a few fabrications. My aims in this book are opposite to those of most modern sociological researchers; taking witchcraft and Satanism as fact, I intend to deal primarily with the practitioners of the black arts themselves, and only tangentially with the motives of the accusers.

Another respect in which this account differs from most modern investigations of such events is that although I feel the structural forms that witchcraft will take will depend to a great extent on social institutions, I believe the core of its existence to lie within the individual psyche. Many reports by ethnologists of the social roots of witchcraft are valid when applied to the cultures under scrutiny but fail the test of truth when applied to the world outside. Similar effects may be the results of different causes, and similar causes might result in different effects. The forms that evolve from analagous social conditions may vary enormously between cultures and between individuals, due to the numerous psychological variables involved. Because of this, any general sociological theory to explain such events is doomed to failure.

Satanism, witchcraft, and mystical secret societies are psychologically related, being rooted in man's constant striving for effectiveness. But although the motivational factors behind such behavior seem to be universally related, it does not follow that these drives are by necessity created and fostered by any one particular type of social organization. To say that witchcraft and Satanism might spring up in times of acute repression, as they did in the Middle Ages in Europe, does not deny the fact that such phenomena may also be generated by cultural fragmentation, which seems to be the case today in America. A multiplicity of social environments may foster in man a feeling of powerlessness, and how he deals with such feelings will inevitably differ between cultures.

The way man handles such a crisis may indeed vary even within a seemingly homogeneous culture, due to the existence of isolated sub-cultures within a society that are conducive to the growth of certain behavior patterns. The cult of Satanists mentioned in Salt Lake City, for example, appears to be a direct outgrowth of and violent reaction against the repressive morality of Mormonism, whereas elsewhere in the United States religious oppression is playing a minor role in the outburst of such activities.

The social and psychological drives motivating any rise in occult activity might channel themselves into non-occult forms as well. There has been a rather short-sighted tendency in the past to treat Satanism and witchcraft as unique phenomena, not having any commonality in either motivation or procedure with any other social organization or group. The irrational basis of these cults has so offended our rational Western way of thinking that those participants indulging in the black arts have seemed to warrant a classification all to themselves. But Satanism, as it has appeared in Western culture, has served those who have felt themselves to be weak and helpless as an escape into power, and in this respect shares the limelight with many other groups fulfilling the same function.

Although the ritualistic proceedings of Satanists might appear alien and terrifying to an outsider, the psychological motivations for the performance of such rites are no harder to understand than the motivations of a Southern Klansman or a German Nazi. All are magical attempts to escape into power. A devout Satanist may be a paranoiac, self-deluded, even dangerous person, and from that point of view may be legitimately considered weird, but I have run across some Klansmen and Nazis whom I would consider stranger and far more dangerous. The black magicians that meet in damp cellars on the day and hour of Saturn to summon those mysterious members of the Descending Hierarchy are indeed captives of their own outlandish hallucinations, but the fact remains that those arcane circles of magicians are no more deluded than clandestine circles such as the Minutemen and the John Birch Society, who conjure infernal demons in the form of fluoridated water or zip codes. Fanaticism in all its guises is undoubtedly scary, but only when it is removed from its isolated existence and put into a broader frame of reference can it become fully understood and therefore dealt with.

There is no doubt in my mind that America is sliding into a period of fragmentary extremism and that the recent growth of Satanism is part of this general trend. A close look beneath the seemingly placid surface of American society reveals the extent to which this process has gone, for the United States is virtually honeycombed with militant clandestine cults. Radical right-wing and leftist conspiratorial groups wield much unseen power in the political spectrum; extremist racial groups, odd religious sects, and bizarre sex cults flourish, meeting and planning action in homes across the country. The prevelance of witchcraft and Satanic covens are a part of this overall proclivity toward cultishness, rather than unique phenomena in themselves. In order to determine how Devil-worship has been able to strike its roots into the soil of American extremism, we must first examine the psychological needs driving these individuals from the middle grounds of society, and then consider how Satanism is able to fill these needs.

The principle cause of the radicalism pervading America today is a growing sense of estrangement on the part of the individual from the prevailing system of values. The United States is rapidly becoming a mass society. Its structure and bewildering complexity are too baffling to be fully understood. Capitalism, while on the one hand providing unprecedented opportunity for the individual to develop to his fullest capacity and vent his creative abilities in the economic sphere, at the same time has tended to reduce a vast majority to the status of cogs in a vast technological complex, stripping them of everything but a market value for their labor. The American that works in a massive industrial complex often is ruled by a boss whom he never sees. He has little decision-making power in matters which effect his fate. Confronted by political machinery that is too gigantic to be responsive to his will, he sees economic and political decisions being made by a select few to whom he has little relevance. Stepping into the streets of overcrowded cities, he is dwarfed by huge billboards advertising toothpaste, nylons, and mouthwash. He sees a military establishment subjecting him and his sons to confusing wars for only dimly understood reasons, the new horrors of war and its finality only adding to the feelings of powerlessness. Stripped and depersonalized, the modern American sees himself as an instrument of society; he has submitted through the process of social heredity and now pays the inevitable price of submission.

The modern American finds himself the incredible shrinking man, growing smaller each day in the face of the unprecedented strides made in technology and communications which have virtually brought the world to his back doorstep. His social frame of reference has increased a billionfold and man finds it suddenly difficult to isolate himself within his culture. His privacy gone, he finds little solace in the anonymous masses which now make up his picture of humanity. The constant exposure to other cultures loosens his firm grasp on his own and he begins to see his position, his moral codes, all that he has held sacred and immutable as relative, not absolute. His tenacious grip on "the truth" is shaken sufficiently to make him stop for a moment and wonder.

The average man is not sufficiently strong to handle this state of uncertainty. At some time in his life, even if but for a brief moment, when his defense mechanisms are lowered, each man sees himself as part of a herd, bland and unspecific. He sees those activities that he thinks are so important for what they really are—activities important perhaps to himself, but totally unimportant to the world around him. Conjuring a mental image of the billions of people in the world who as functioning units are just as important as himself, he realizes that they are not even conscious of his existence. Stripped of his uniqueness, man views himself as being isolated and useless, living a life devoid of meaning. No longer knowing who he is, man stands listlessly on a dimly lighted street corner, waiting for some stranger to come by and supply the answer.

The original safety valves, such as religion and the secular moral codes of society, which have traditionally handled the "bleeding-off" of such neurotic symptoms, have become broken down in the face of the new technology. Man has landed on the moon, but half-empty churches still echo the same tired rhetoric expressed in the same tired fashion that has been heard for centuries. The old religious and moral values seem to have become irrelevant to man and his needs, needs which they were at one time able to fill. The old concepts of Heaven and Hell have become anachronisms, useless tools which man has forgotten how to use. The gap between knowledge and values has widened to such an extent that it has become almost unbridgeable. The crying need for a new order has arisen, but until man is able to erect a new set of values by which he may order his universe, he must continue to grope chaotically in the dark, finding comfort where he can.

Man has often tried to convince himself that he is able to live without religion, but the louder he has shouted, the more these protestations have sounded like the whistling of a frightened man in the dark. He may be able to get along very well without organized religion, but "religion," as far as identification with something higher than oneself, either with a god or even with a secular cause, is indispensable. Religion as an emotional process, as a reassurance to each individual that his actions are indeed important, is an attempt to achieve a feeling of timelessness and permanence in a world of flux.

Religion as such may take on many forms. Religious experience may be gained from the ritualizing of one's own actions, by making a fetish of one's daily work routine, a trait found frequently in modern Americans; it may be sought in an emotional involvement with another person, such as love; it may possibly be achieved through identification with a militant political or religious group, or in a mystical tribal sharing in the expansive wondrousness of mankind as a whole.

All religious and political movements acquire and maintain adherents through their manipulation of symbols. By impregnating himself with the symbols of ritual, bizarre as those symbols may be, the celebrant is able to transcend his immediate self and become part of a timeless, permanent universe. Satan as a symbol holds great attraction for many of those now finding their lives depleted of religious symbolism, for there has always been a little Satan in all of us. He is lazy at times, aggressive at times, prideful, rebellious, deceitful, arrogant, lustful, greedy, and, as such, is a much closer approximation of man than the omnipotent and perfect Judeo-Christian God. In today's secular age, when Christian symbolism is rapidly losing its force and vitality, it is natural that the rallying symbols of the opposition should take over.

Religion, then, in the sense meant here, is a means by which the individual identifies with these symbols which lend meaning to his otherwise dry, insipid existence. This definition differs significantly from the definitions of anthropologists who have limited the scope of religion in order that they might have a usable tool for cultural analyses. I am purposely blurring the defining lines to provide a closer approximation to reality. The increasingly magical flavor which is seeping into Satanism today is not contradictory in the least with the idea of religion, but, in fact, is complementary to it. Aleister Crowley emphasized this point in his definitions of evocation and invocation, that the goals of higher magic and religion are at base identical, the culmination of ritual being *samahdi*, the total immersion of self in godhead.

But higher magic and religion are not only similar in goal, but also bear striking likenesses in procedure, the rituals of both being based on rhythm and repetition. The Black Mass, the demonic conjurations, the invocations and paeans offered to Lucifer, the hymns sung, the strange chanting, all facilitate the loss of ego within the group. They all provide a means of complete and final identification with the symbol of worship. Their hypnotic quality tends to loosen the grip held on man by his conscious mind and, shaking him free of the burdensome constraints of society, temporarily enables him to lapse into animality. Political demagogues and successful preachers are true magicians in this sense, for they are able to manipulate the masses by the use of slogans, symbols, and chants.

The old distinction made by ethnologists between magic and religion is superfluous in many respects, for no act is purely religious or purely magical. Both practices are born out of the same psychological need, the need to feel oneself a meaningful, effective individual. The magician is able to feel unique and effective in the practice of his craft because he is manipulating what he sees to be universal forces, and as such is elevating himself to the level of the divine. The religious devotee is able to put himself in a similarly advantageous position, for in attaining what he feels to be a "state of grace," he is able to transcend the normal stream of life and merge with the celestial.

The tiresome distinctions between religious "supplication" and magical "manipulation" are so much wasted effort, for in most of the Satanist groups which I have encountered, even those with the purist magical flavor, the participants virtually *submit to ritual*. They purposely strive for a state of ego-loss within the group through the use of ritual, their approach to magic being therefore religious in the true Crowleyan sense.

The search for some higher meaning that pervades man's existence is Protean and constantly changes form. But one common thread linking all those possible forms is the need for attachment, for only by relating to other people may man achieve a feeling of identity. Attachment, in its more normal aspects, manifests itself in human affection. In its more neurotic forms, it tends to degenerate into a self-immolating dependence, in which the object or symbol of attachment is adopted out of a need to escape from oneself and from the world in general. The attachment in this case is an attempt by the neurotic to build a fantasy world, a magical land of enchantment in which he may find refuge from those upsetting, frustrating relationships encountered in the outside world.

As we have seen, Satanism in the Middle Ages, growing up as it did under a brutally oppressive social system, displayed this self-immolating quality. By attaching themselves to the group, the witches achieved security through identification. The old Satanism was more than merely a ritual rebellion against the prevailing power structure, for it was an attempt to escape the disturbing breakdown of traditional values brought by the invading Christianity. One cannot indefinitely run, he must run *somewhere*. When Hughes described the Sabbat as a "barbaric release into an even earlier worship," he was quite correct, for early Satanism was in a sense a nativistic movement, an attempt to retreat into familiarity and order, to restore the paganism of the pre-Christian era.

Some of the new extremist groups in America, including some modern Satanist cults, reflect this tendency, in essence being attempts to escape the current breakdown in values that is being generated by a complex, confusing technology. The search is on in all parts of American culture for a Messiah, for a symbol strong enough to lead man out of the chaotic, swirling darkness. Analogous in many respects to the Satanism of Medieval Europe are some of the more clandestine reactionary political groups operating in the United States today, and many of these groups have multiplied their memberships with alarming speed in the last few years. The goals of the KKK, the John Birch Society, the Minutemen and others to restore America, by any means possible, to a state of simplicity and purity are not a far cry from these Satanists encountered by Seabrook in New York who were trying through their Black Masses to "restore Lucifer to the throne of the universe" in order to re-establish peace and harmony. The forms in which a need for attachment is institutionalized may be varied, changing with a change in social conditions and depending on the psychological leanings of the individuals involved, but basically they are often interchangeable.

Although the overt authoritarianism of the old Satanism is still in operation in some Satanic covens in the form of ritual prostration and even physical sado-masochism, much of the debasing procedures are being purged from the ceremonies. The current emphasis on ceremonial magic as a way of communicating with deity is lending a seemingly different air to the rituals. During some ceremonies which I attended, a rather intimate approach to the Prince of Darkness was taken; the members conjured the Devil as a spiritualist would during a seance conjure a departed friend or relative. Satan is beginning to lose his frightening appearance and to take on all the aspects of a "Dear Abby" of the underworld. This trend is evidence of an undeniable separation-anxiety, of a crying need on the part of these people for affection, the need to identify with a powerful friend. However much the overt sado-masochism seems to be absent from the rituals, the neurotic dependence on the group is still at work, if at a more subtle level.

Very strong ties are apparent within Satanic covens, the members that I interviewed expressing a great personal attachment to the group as a means of identification. When speaking about the group, they seemed to express feelings of superiority over non-members. They all had that I-know-something-you-don't-know glint in their eyes, a look carried by all true believers who think that they have acquired powers not normally found in outsiders. When separated from the coven, however, and engaged in normal conversation, I found most to be suffering from acute feelings of inferiority. Their illusions of strength seem to be rooted firmly within the boundaries of the group and seldom extend beyond those limits.

As an example of this extreme dependence on the group as a source of strength, one day I happened to be discussing astral projection with a young Satanist, a practice employed extensively in this particular coven's rituals. He related to me that he had found it quite exhilarating, but that most of the people he had encountered were frightened by the thought of the experience. He asked me if I had ever tried it, and I replied that I had, but that I had not been very successful, attributing my failure to my rather carnal attachment to my body. I told him that the only fear I would have of achieving a state of mind projection would be that some other person in the astral state might be waiting to enter my body when I was out of it, and thus displace my own personality. At this remark, he looked down despondently and muttered that that fear had never entered his mind, due to the fact that *nobody would want his body!*

I could see his point, although I restrained myself from telling him so. He was of runtish build and had long, stringy hair; his face displayed a nice collection of pimples and he wore thick glasses to compensate for his defective eyesight. His jaunts into astral projection were obviously welcome relief from the insecurities of normalcy. They were an escape from a physical realm he found to be a burden rather than a pleasure. The fact that such an attitude is completely contradictory to Satan as a symbol of carnality and material existence did not seem to bother him in the least. The participation in the coven and its rituals was the important thing for this individual; the rest could be reconciled or not reconciled at his leisure. The group provided him with a sense of strength and adequacy which he singularly lacked on the outside.

One reason that these cults are able to furnish the feelings of power that they do is precisely for this reason. They serve as vehicles by which the members may vent their frustrations with the outside world. It has been said that secret societies and minority groups have often become the scapegoats for the failures and jealousies of the prevailing social system. This is undoubtedly true, as can be seen from the persecution of the early witches by the Inquisition. The Jewish minorities of Europe and the Negro minorities of America have also often served as whipping-boys for the powerful majorities. But during such periods of persecution, group solidarity invariably increases, and often a strong reaction formation sets in. The present "Black is beautiful" slogan of militant Negroes and the orthodox Jewish social prohibitions against exogamy are examples of this kind of reaction formation.

Even though the witchcraft persecutions died out long ago, this inverted scapegoating of society for the feelings of failure and inadequacy within the groups has continued, and has provided a source of strength for many joiners. Blaming the outside for their anxieties, the members turn to the group to find power, and these feelings of inner-group superiority increase proportionally to the sense of estrangement felt for the outside.

One factor aiding group solidarity and acting as an attraction for many potential converts is the esoteric nature of the cults. By being the inheritors of such an admittedly colorful tradition, by partaking in the emotionally stirring and often animalistic rituals, the disciples are able to feel themselves apart from the body of humanity.

Such feelings of uniqueness are intensified by the degree of secrecy prevailing among the cults. Secrecy lends an aura of mystery to the proceedings and radiates an alluring magnetism. A secret is a personal possession, an extension of oneself. Having such a possession, one which seemingly very few others have, reinforces those feelings of superiority and power that the individual seeks to acquire. In this rather unprivate and open society, being able to have something so private has great appeal for many who find themselves becoming more and more depersonalized.

Secrecy goes hand in hand with another closely related, although not identical, concept—inaccessibility. Both, however, seem to be operating within the Satanic covens to fill the psychological craving for possession. Once the split from the outside has been accomplished, once all the doors have been slammed shut and tightly sealed, the member may feel snug and secure in his warm little refuge. The more exclusive the member feels his group to be, the more it becomes a possession, a personal mark of achievement. This craving is not limited solely to secret societies. To see what a powerful motivating force this quest for possession is in our modern American culture, all one has to do is look at the lengths to which some of the "depersonalized rich" will go, the exorbitant prices they will pay, to secure admittance into ultra-exclusive country clubs.

When secrecy and inaccessibility are coupled with the esoteric nature of Satanism, its strange and compelling ritual, the group becomes an interlocking whole, and the feelings of power and warmth generated within are enhanced accordingly. The ultimate goal of the Satanist is a new self. He seeks to rejuvenate himself by immersing himself in a higher power.

But strangely enough, the very secrecy and inaccessibility under which the groups operate, while in many cases being the honey which has brought the bees to the hive, is also a factor acting to retard any large-scale coordination between groups. As long as the extreme paranoia within the movement exists, the prospects of any massive, well-planned assault on modern society are quite dim. Indeed, if the groups managed to convert themselves into a mass movement, and were thus put into a position where they had to incorporate all elements of the population into their ranks, they might well lose their exclusive appeal.

If, then, modern Satanism is the result of a massive alienation from the value system as it now stands, then those making up the brunt of the movement should come from the most disaffected elements of society, those suffering most from feelings of isolation and estrangement.

The rise of witchcraft practices is often a gauge of man's economic and social condition. Those having the hardest time finding a place within society are those most likely to search for effectiveness outside the social realm. In the history of witchcraft and Satanism, those most frequently accused of vile practices were women, especially of the lower classes. Women in the days of the Inquisition were the most oppressed element of society; they were the weakest segment of the population economically, politically, and socially. Denied psychological effectiveness through the prevailing system, they turned inevitably to more esoteric sources of strength, and Satan, a great egalitarian, welcomed them with open arms.

Today the worshippers of Satan are similarly those who feel themselves unable to come to grips with the social system as it stands. But it has become a religion of only a certain element of the disaffected. It has acquired few followers among rural populations, among the poor, or among the illiterate.

The apparent absence of Satanism in rural areas demonstrates a definite correlation between the anxieties engendered by a mass culture and the current rise of Devilworship. Only in the metropolitan cities of the United States do such practices take place in an organized form. In rural areas, superstition and magical practices tend to be more innocuous, being performed by individuals rather than groups, and usually are used to effect more limited, utilitarian ends. Water-witching and divining are common examples of this pragmatic rural magic. Rituals are never performed merely for the sake of ritual, but for a particular purpose, to heal the sick, find water, predict the outcome of a planting, procure a lover, etc. This type of witchcraft is due more to a lack of understanding of the forces of nature, to a technology gap, than it is to any deep-seated psychological insecurity on the part of the operator. Superstition is a product of ignorance. Satanism is a product of desperation.

In the great metropolitan centers, where man ironically finds himself most alone among millions of people, where he is a meaningless speck of humanity, bumped and shoved and manipulated by concerns that are not even aware of his existence, the attachment to a group and to ritual become ends for their own sake, and pragmatic ends are forced into the back seat. It is not surprising, then, that the focus of power in the Satanic movement lies in such sprawling industrial cities as New York, Detroit, Los Angeles, and Philadelphia.

Satanism has made its greatest inroads among the educated upper and middle classes for several reasons. Satanism lost its lower-class component at the end of the sixteenth century and has not regained it. The Satanism of the peasantry was a reaction against Christianity; the Satanism of the aristocracy was a reaction against boredom. Since the ties between poverty and religion have been severed, the dissatisfaction of the poor has tended to be vented in political rather than religious terms. The purpose in joining a Satanic coven today is not to obtain wealth or riches, as for many peasants in the Middle

Ages; the purpose is to find a relief, however temporary, from the pangs of disaffection.

That Satanism has been popular primarily among the educated stems from its historical development among the upper classes. As it evolved from the minds of an intelligentsia, the rituals of Satanism have been traditionally complex. The abstract symbology employed in much of the ceremony has often been far above the grasp of the ignorant. The singular attraction Satanism has held for the illiterate has been its historical sexual image.

Obviously not all middle-class, educated city dwellers are Satanists, or even potential Satanists. There are more potential Satanists among these groups, however, than among other groups. Those making most likely converts are those who feel alienated, those who are desperately seeking to refill their lives with symbolic meaning. Three such segments of society, which at this time seem to make up the brunt of the Satanic movement, are the young, the bored, and the misfits.

Satanism today is a comparatively young movement. The type of youth I have found to be most frequently involved is overly sensitive and basically passive in nature. Many are of the rebellious, long-haired variety, who are seemingly prone to reckless experimentation. This inclination to experimentation, however, is seldom particularly courageous, and more often than not is self-destructive, taking the form of a search for a source of external rather than internal strength. When conversing with these young people I got a distinct feeling of passivity, that they wanted things to happen *to* them rather than being the initiators of action. Drug use was frequent in the rituals of these groups, this being a primary reason why these young people found Satanism so attractive. Since most of them were drug-users before entering the coven, it was easy for them to make the group identification. Already identifying with a subculture that uses psychedelics, it would be difficult for a member to switch allegiance to a reference group opposed to their use. Identity-transfer is facilitated among groups with a similar orientation, it being unnecessary to make a complete break from a former way of life.

Hallucinogens have played a major role in the development of Satanism and they have special relevance when one considers the present composition of the Satanic membership. As stated earlier, religious experience may be substituted for organized religion in the minds of men, and the increasing use of drugs in this country indicates, to some extent at least, that such an attempted substitution is taking place. Timothy Leary, the so-called "high priest" of the psychedelic movement, roughly serves in this capacity, as a guide for those wishing to partake in the mystical side of religious experience. Psychedelics are professed by leaders such as Leary to be roads to enlightenment, means of attaining "spiritual truth."

The availability of narcotics seems to be one deterministic factor in outbreaks of magic and Satanism. Many of the stronger drugs have a permanent dissociative effect on the human mind, and in this sense it may be said that hallucinogens are the father of Satan. Magicians have traditionally made free use of narcotics in their ceremonies for obvious reasons. It is much easier to materialize a demon from the depths of one's own mind than it is to summon one all the way from Hell.

Traditionally, before attempting a conjuration, the operator is supposed to prepare himself by abstaining from food or drink and by a purposeful lack of sleep. With the body in a weakened state, the mind is more susceptible to auto-suggestion, and thus the magical operation is more likely to be successful. Some modern magicians recommend an opposite procedure—namely, self-indulgence to the point of mild exhaustion. Sexual intercourse and alcohol are employed by these sorcerers before and sometimes during a conjuration. Many of the substances burned and inhaled by the magicians during the rituals have hallucinogenic properties. Hemlock, henbane, and opium are some of the narcotics traditionally used. During the Black Masses described by Huysmans, hashish was abundantly burned in place of incense. It is not surprising to note that in many of the accounts given by sorcerers, the demons that they supposedly materialized have been described as "bringers of light," particularly since many of the drugs used render the eyes particularly sensitive to light and color.

Due to the difficulty in obtaining more traditional narcotics such as hemlock and henbane, most of the newer cults burn quantities of hashish during their ceremonies. I accompanied one Satanist to several supermarkets one night in an urgent search for lard. Upon returning to his home, we were met by a few members of the coven, who helped him grind up tannis root in an electric blender. Although he did not tell me what the lard was for, I could pretty well deduce its purpose. The tannis root and lard are used as a base for a psychedelic ointment that is roughly analogous to the "flying ointment" used by the old witches of Europe. This coven was composed almost entirely of young hippie types (for lack of a better descriptive term) who were seeking, through the use of hallucinogens, a release into a religious world.

The young, says Eric Hoffer, are susceptible to proselytizing movements, religious and political, due to the fact that they are "temporary misfits," people who feel that they have not yet found their place in life but who are impatiently searching. The young Satanists seem most often to be from that element of American youth which feels itself pressured; dissatisfied with the social values of preceding generations, they are searching elsewhere for an answer. The prevalent use of drugs among them is merely one manifestation of this restlessness and dissatisfaction. They seem to carry about with them an electric desperation; driven by the fear that the best part of their lives might be wasted before they finally find their place in life, they attach themselves to any symbol which might furnish them with some identity. At some of the Satanic rituals I attended, their credulity, their apparent wish to believe was truly amazing to behold; the most ludicrous carnival tricks were lapped up without the least bit of skepticism.

Some of the new Satanic groups, particularly those still oriented toward sex, are ruled by the bored, those people who have grown up in the culture to find their social and religious existences to contain the seeds of apathy.

One segment of the bored most susceptible to the perverse side of Satanism is the middle-class suburbanite who craves an escape from the sterile uniformity of his plastic tract home, from the dull routine of Sunday barbecues, and the monotonous drone of weekly bridge parties. Having little recourse to privacy, trapped in a network of meaningless and superficial relationships which tend to diminish rather than increase feelings of uniqueness and personal adequacy, the middle-class suburbanite is a potential convert to any esoteric, secretive cause which promises to spice up the daily routine of living, as long as it does not at the same time have an adverse effect on his economic and social position. The disaffection among this section of the population is evidenced by the astounding growth of deviant sex patterns among such people, such as wife-swapping clubs.

One might expect to find among such groups a pattern emerging that differs not too drastically from the old Hellfire Clubs, which were born out of basically the same needs. This is, in fact, what is happening. According to occultist E. J. Gold, "It is common knowledge that wife-swapping clubs are increasingly being converted into Satanic covens. The growing interest in the supernatural, the flair for the exotic shared by the members of these clubs, the sexual preoccupation of historical Satanism, all act to facilitate the conversion."

Sex is a predominant force within these groups for the reason that the participants are still bound in part to the old morality. Sex to them is a rebellion against the boredom of their lives, and as such is a reaction against what they see to be the prevailing system of ethics. It is an excursion into a forbidden land, an attempt to transcend the world of mediocrity in which they find themselves and to erect a fantasy world of perversion into which they may periodically escape.

Pure self-indulgence, however, seldom supplies the meaning sought by the participants. The original stimulation that such immoral activities provided soon wears off, and man again begins to lapse into ennui. This is where Satanism comes in. "Two choices are left to the individual who finds himself in the position where he has exhausted all the possible combinations of a limited membership," states Gold. "He either brings in new members, increasing the boundaries of the circle, which is potentially dangerous to his social position, or he attempts to add ceremonial elements to his perversions, to inculcate a religious meaning. The growing influence of Satanism among such groups is indicative of the latter trend." According to Gold, the rites celebrated by the wife-swapping Satanists are more traditional, due to their sexual nature. In such groups, the Black Mass has survived, its distorted remnants being torn from the pages of old Dennis Wheatley novels.

Such sex-oriented groups are perhaps the most unstable element in the Satanic ranks, their dedication being more to sex than to the concept of Satan. The celebrants are simply looking for an excuse, *any* excuse for an orgy. Anton LaVey, in a recent article for *The Insider,* described the activities of one such cult that he witnessed in the Echo Park area in Los Angeles, near Amy Semple MacPherson's famous Angelus Temple. The "Satanic" High Priest presiding over the celebration was the prototype of the "dirty old man," dressed in white robes and sandals. The congregation, about twenty in number, were predominantly young hippies, but other elements were represented. "Acid" was distributed to the congregation. The room used was black and black candles were burned. The altar was, according to LaVey, the most conspicuous part of the room, and probably the most laughable. It consisted of a long table, on one end of which was a statue of a nude man, sporting an oversized, Day-Glo-red penis. On the other end was the statue of a nude woman, with her nipples and vagina painted in an equally conspicuous manner. The proceedings got under way when the priest read excerpts from Waite's *Book of Ceremonial Magic*, followed by Crowley's "Hymn to Pan." The old man then proceeded to explain to the congregation what sexual acrobatics they were to go through in order to achieve communion with godhead. LaVey went on to state that it was obvious that the entire affair was staged merely for the benefit of the high priest, who sat watching the ensuing orgy greedily, in order that he get his degenerate "kicks" through vicarious participation.

Misfits constitute a minority of all those who presently call themselves Satanists, but in contributing heavily to the more hard-core, radical cults, they often receive a disproportionate share of the publicity. These are the out-and-out sadists and masochists, the perverts and degenerates, whose exploits are picked up avidly by sensationalism-hungry magazines. These are the elements usually linked in the popular mind with Satanism, the tones responsible for the barbaric animal sacrifices, the sadistic beatings, the acts of necrophilia, and the ritual murders that have received wide exposure in the national and local press. These are the people who feel themselves compelled toward violence, who feel so alienated from the social system that they can see no hope of ever returning.

The alienation experienced by such misfits is cumulative, growing more acute the longer they find themselves unable to express themselves through normal channels. Unable to relate meaningfully to others and to conventionality, they displace the hatred they hold for themselves onto the system to which they have been unable to adjust. The misfits search for an appropriate symbol to embody their pent-up emotions, and Satan, the adversary, the champion of all misfits, stands in the eaves, waiting for his cue.

The Los Angeles group of Satanists [mentioned earlier] that practices extortion in order to maintain group solidarity is an example of the attraction the name "Satan" holds for these hard-core elements. The ritualistic proceedings in this cult are highly sado-masochistic at a physical level, scourgings and other such practices providing entertainment for the congregations. The two leaders of this group are homosexuals. Parolees and ex-convicts make up a disproportionate percentage of its initiates.

Such groups are comparatively rare, but the potential appeal they hold for outcasts is undoubtedly great. Anton LaVey admitted to me that he receives a great number of letters from convicts whose releases from prison are pending, applying for membership into the Church of Satan. Although LaVey invariably disregards these letters, the fact remains that the prisoners writing him do not know that he will. Their limited knowledge of the group is drawn from the gaudy publicity devoted to the Church in "girlie magazines"; they are attracted to what they think is a deviant, anti-social, sexual movement—a perfect vehicle for ritualizing the hatred they feel for the society that has coldly excluded them. A movement geared to their tastes, however, could capitalize on the seething resentment that they hold for the established system, and could find a willing and pliable audience in these baser social types. Taking into consideration the phenomenal skyrocketing of crime rates in recent years, the rising rate of homosexuality, and the growing number of neurotics and psychotics, these misfits could prove to be a major future market for the more extreme Satanist cults.

And the level of violence seems to be increasing with each passing day. One trend that seems to be occurring is the transition of Eric Hoffer's young, "temporary misfits" into the ranks of the more violent, permanent misfits. One reason for this is that these young, fervently anti-Establishment people, strongly influenced by drug-use, are easily manipulated by psychotic, overbearing personalities, as apparently was the case in the Charles Manson Family.

Recently, authorities around the Santa Cruz area of California have reported that they have been receiving reports of strange rituals being held in the Santa Cruz mountains, a haven for hippie communes. Informants have told police that they have attended "witchcraft meetings" at which animals were sacrificed and humans were turned into the "slaves of Satan." One man told about participating in fire dances and blood-drinking rituals at Boulder Creek, near Santa Cruz, and stated that glue-sniffing was part of the ceremony. Another young man reported to police that he had seen a group of hippies dancing wildly around a parked car, on the hood of which were the carcasses of five skinned dogs. Verification of this strange story came from the Santa Cruz Community Animal Shelter, which reported that during the past eighteen months there have turned up in the area bodies of a number of skinned dogs. The skinning had been expertly done, the skin having been cut away on all the animals "without even marking the flesh." A sidelight is that all the animals had been drained of their blood. Other barbaric practices have been reported to local authorities. Teenagers in the Santa Cruz area have described initiation rituals during which the neophytes are forced to eat the entrails of an animal "while its heart is still beating."

Most of the informants have stated that they were initiated while under the influence of hallucinogenic drugs. It seems that the leaders of the group gain power over the members, impressing them with their "supernatural powers," thus instilling the proper amount of fear to insure obedience while their minds are in this malleable state. The omnipresent desperation, the sadistic will to subjugate, and the masochistic will to be enslaved are all present in such groups. The violently anti-social proclivities of these elements and their typically mystical sense of perception, which is aided by their frequent use of hallucinogenic drugs, is likely to lead to a spiralling pattern of barbarity. The participants in these rites, in abjectly surrendering themselves to any magnetic leader who calls himself Satan, are cutting themselves off completely from the outside world, and are increasingly entering the world of the permanent misfit.

Dr. Arnold Wilson, a Los Angeles psychiatrist who is currently conducting research into the new upsurge of occultism in the United States, told me that he found the rise of such activities in the past three years to be very disturbing. He attributes the current rise of witchcraft and Satanism to the increasingly rapid rate of technology and saw the prevalence of wars and the political unrest on college campuses all as being symptomatic of the fragmentation of values brought about by rapid technological change. "The culture is no longer able to work," he stated. "The whole culture is becoming fragmented. Using, say, Toynbee's theory of the birth, growth, and necessary death of civilizations, if placed on a graph, we would be somewhere on the decline."

As pessimistic as this may sound, it is perhaps an uncomfortable yet inescapable truth. Changes will have to be made if the fabric of society is to be preserved, changes both in our social institutions and within each of us as individuals.

THE JESUS MOVEMENT: THE RESURGENCE OF MIRACLES

After rediscovering mystery through the use of drugs, after finding the magical aspects inherent in witchcraft, astrology, transcendental meditation, and other forms of Eastern religion, what was there left for the counter-culture to discover? Of all things, it turned out to be Jesus.

In a two-week-long period of revival in California eleven thousand people came forward to declare themselves for Jesus. In a single parade in Chicago over a thousand young people were converted. These were not individuals carried away with mass hysteria, because days after their conversions they were baptized and became publically committed to Jesus.[1] Such converts now number in the hundreds of thousands, but because the decision is private and the numbers are growing rapidly, it is impossible accurately to estimate the current "Jesus" population. Jesus people are officially organized on nearly every major college campus. Growth, organization, and proselytization seem to characterize these groups.

In addition to Jesus people on campus, Jesus freaks organize communally. It is estimated that there are two hundred Jesus communes in California alone[2] and perhaps as many as four hundred throughout the country. These communes base their lives on the Book of Acts, and their lives are often highly regimented.[3] Since their intention is to emulate the life of Christ they preach against the use of drugs and

1. "The Jesus Revolution—Miracle in Young America?" in *The Readers Digest,* 99 (December 1971), 135–38.
2. "Street Christians: Jesus as the Ultimate Trip," in *Time* magazine, 96 (August 1970), 31–32.
3. "The Jesus People," in *Newsweek,* 77 (March 1971), 97.

sex outside of marriage.[4] The movement represents a fundamentalist Christianity that has not demythologized religion.

However, if there is any distinguishing characteristic of the members of the Jesus movement, it is not their fundamentalism or the size of the movement, but rather the intensity of their belief in a supernatural, awesome Jesus Christ who is not just a man but a living God. Their lives are centered on an intense personal relationship with Jesus. They act as if divine intervention guides their behavior and can be counted on to solve every problem.[5] Finally, the movement shares the conviction of early Christianity that Doomsday is very near.[6]

Most of the members of the Jesus movement feel the movement itself is a miraculous movement—an intervention of God in human history—and a movement that emphasizes the daily, miraculous intervention of Jesus into the lives of its members. With regard to the miraculous nature of the movement itself, their reasoning proceeds along these lines: There are many scriptures in the Bible that prophesy the signs of the end of the world. First, there will be famines (Matthew 24:7); members point to the hunger that already exists in Biafra, India, Pakistan, and some parts of the United States. There will be earthquakes (Luke 21:11); to document this sign, they point to California, Japan, Chile, and Peru. The recapture of old Jerusalem is interpreted as another sign (Zachariah 12–14 and Ezekiel 36:16–18). Wars (Matthew 24:6), rioting (Luke 21:25), and the peace movement (I Thessalonians 3:5) are other events that Jesus people claim are signs of the end. However, there are two more important signs. First, the Jesus movement itself is a precursor that some members claim was predicted in the second chapter of Joel. Second, preceding the return of Jesus and the end of the world there will be an outpouring of the Holy Spirit upon all men. To bring that prediction to fruition is the ultimate purpose for which God has created the Jesus movement.

However, besides this final cosmic miracle, the members strongly believe that Jesus often performs personal miracles of purification. Through belief in Jesus and following His will, many have themselves been—or seen others who have been—saved from a life of promiscuous drugs or sex. Their attitudinal changes have been dramatic and therefore interpreted as miraculous. This real belief in personal miracles is in sharp contrast to the continued deemphasis of miracles in the institutional church.

Stark and Glock, in a California survey, found that only slightly more than half of all Protestants sampled (57 percent) believed that

4. "Street Christians," p. 31.
5. "The Jesus Revolution," p. 136.
6. "Street Christians," p. 32.

the miracles described in the Bible actually happened.[7] Hadden found in a national survey of ministers that only 28 percent of Methodists, 40 percent of Episcopalians, and 36 percent of Presbyterians agreed that the birth of Jesus was a biological miracle.[8] The Jesus movement came along in a decidedly unmiraculous age.

However, there are other items of doctrine in which members of the Jesus movement believe that are not salient to large numbers of church members.

Jesus people strongly believe in the Second Coming. In contrast, only 44 percent of all Protestants definitely believe that Jesus will return, although as many as 94 percent of Southern Baptists believe this is true.

Jesus people believe that Jesus walked on water, while only 50 percent of all Protestants believe that Jesus actually performed this miracle. Again, Southern Baptists almost unanimously (99 percent) believe this to be true.

Jesus people definitely believe in the divinity of Jesus, in contrast to 69 percent of all Protestants. However, Southern Baptists again are almost unanimous (99 percent) in their belief in the divinity of Jesus.

An analysis of these findings suggests that the Jesus movement is more closely allied in belief with the fundamentalist ideology present in some mainline churches.

The Jesus movement began quietly in California sometime in 1967 with a few people banding together to worship, having found that traditional churches did not meet their spiritual needs. From the beginning there has been neither an individual spokesman nor a great deal of cohesion to it. In fact, the Jesus movement really did not become a movement until sometime in late 1969 or early 1970, when it captured the attention of the media. Since that time it has been the subject of numerous magazine articles and television documentaries, most of which have, on the one hand, enhanced its appeal and credibility among the young (making it a movement) and, on the other hand, obscured the diversity of the movement itself.

The most recent development in the history of the movement occurred in Dallas in July of 1972, the scene of Explo 72. Hundreds of thousands of young people who were not in the movement two years ago and many of the original Jesus freaks converged on Dallas to learn about Jesus, to learn about how to spread His word effectively, and to witness to His importance in their lives.

7. Rodney Stark and Charles Y. Glock, *American Piety: The Nature of Religious Commitment* (Berkeley: University of California Press, 1968), pp. 27–41.

8. Jeffrey K. Hadden, *The Gathering Storm in the Churches* (Garden City, New York: Anchor Books, 1969), p. 55.

Since it became a matter on the public agenda, perhaps the most often asked question about the Jesus movement has been—is it just another fad? Or, put another way, if the movement lasts how will the churches deal with it? After Explo 72, perhaps the answers to these questions are clearer. The Jesus movement has moved into another phase. The main core of its membership now looks different and has an entirely different biographical background from the California members of just a few years ago. The new members are increasingly "straight." They are respectable college and high-school students, actively affiliated with a denomination, and without sordid past histories of drugs and sex. In addition, the organizer of Explo 72, Bill Bright, and the main speaker, the Reverend Billy Graham, are emerging as spokesmen for the movement. They are attempting to do what they have done most successfully in the past—that is, organize the movement and mediate between it and the traditional churches. From one perspective this is viewed as a positive stage of the movement: free-floating movements can not endure long. Yet from another it looks like the coopting of the movement by those who, under the aegis of revivalism, recruit members for the traditional churches.

Whether or not this effort will be successful is doubtful. The reason is clear. The Jesus movement differs from churchly Christianity in both its style and its intensity. The Jesus movement is a primary example of the resurgence of the miraculous in American religion.

At this point, the future of the Jesus movement is undetermined. Whatever course the movement takes it will have a profound impact on American Christianity. If any of the mainline churches succeed in coopting the movement, it will be the fundamentalists. It is their common ideology that has the potential for uniting the Jesus movement and the fundamentalists. However, if the Jesus movement continues to be disaffiliated with the churches, then neither the Jesus movement nor the churches themselves will have a significant impact on American culture. Bumper stickers, honking your horn for Jesus, being stoned on Jesus, and loving your enemy because it will drive him crazy are not the stuff out of which lasting movements arise.

Aside from its transience as a popular movement, the Jesus movement is most often criticized for its facile solutions to social ills. In the last analysis, the miracles that Jesus people depend upon to solve complex problems perhaps undermine the social bonds that created and support the movement.

The first reading in this section is "The Jesus Generation." In this paper I attempt to delineate some of the social conditions that are related to the development of the Jesus generation and to distinguish between three distinct but related levels of the Jesus movement. The first and broadest level is that of the religious themes in the entire youth culture. The second level is that of specifically religious youth movements, and the third level is that of radical religious movements within the Jesus movement.

The next paper is within the first level of analysis—the Jesus movement as an element of popular culture. More specifically, it attempts to understand and explain the phenomenon of *Jesus Christ Superstar*. This reading, "*Sgt. Pepper, Hair,* and *Tommy,*" by Patrick Morrow, analyzes the musical forerunners of *Superstar*. Morrow does not see the Jesus-Rock movement as a new direction for popular music; rather, he argues that *Superstar* is the musical fulfillment of ideas presented in the *Sgt. Pepper* album, in the musical *Hair,* and in the Who's rock opera, *Tommy.* The irony of Morrow's contention is that each of these musical productions has at one time or another been thought to be antithetical to religion, Christianity, and Jesus.

"Mainlining Jesus: The New Trip" reports on one of the few surveys to be conducted on Jesus people. Adams and Fox provide some basic demographic and psychological data from their small survey of Jesus people in California. The authors describe the movement and conclude by criticizing it for its conservative politics, simplistic view of human nature, lack of social concern, and denial of the importance of the future. They do concede, however, that the Jesus communes are the most impressive part of this social movement.

The final selection is concerned with Jesus communes—those radical religious organizations that present the greatest reason for hope and considerable reason to fear the outcome of the Jesus movement. Enroth, Ericson, and Peters describe such communes as the "Children of God" and Tony Alamo's "Foundation" as the epitome of the movement. They are disturbed, however, by their cultic isolation from the rest of the movement. In the end, because this level of the movement is the least faddish, it can be expected to last longer and have a more significant impact on American religion. Nevertheless, the intensity of the impact of the Jesus communes might ultimately depend on their acceptance or rejection by traditional Christians.

THE JESUS GENERATION

Edward F. Heenan

IT HAS BEEN ALMOST TEN YEARS SINCE THE ANNOUNCEMENT OF THE "death of God" by theologians Altizer, Van Buren, and Hamilton.[1] We were told that his death was not "unexpected" and that he died "during major surgery to correct a massive diminishing influence." [2] The news was traumatic to those who had believed in him so strongly. Others were less affected, recognizing in this startling proclamation a profound need not to eliminate the concept of God, but simply to change his image. Still others, whose credentials are unquestioned but whose investment in religion was minimal, found evidence for the dawn of a post-Christian era.[3]

With the aid of hindsight, it would seem that these predictions were, for the most part, premature. Unless one is extremely selective about what he admits as evidence, it seems clear that the concepts of God and religion are still alive in the minds of the majority of Americans. It seems equally clear, however, that the packaging of the image of God has changed in the last decade. Rather than focusing on a God "out there," the emphasis recently has been on the incarnate or immanent deity. In the Western religious tradition this means Jesus.

Jesus began his rise from association with a moribund God

"The Jesus Generation," by Edward F. Heenan. Copyright © 1973 by Edward F. Heenan. This article appears for the first time in this volume. Printed by permission of the author.

This essay is a revised copy of a paper presented at the Society for the Study of Popular Culture, April 1972.

1. Harvey Cox, "The Death of God and the Future of Theology," in William Robert Miller, ed., *The New Christianity* (New York: Delacorte Press, 1967), pp. 377–89.

2. Anthony Towne, "God is Dead in Georgia," *Motive*, February 1966.

3. Rodney Stark and Charles Y. Glock, *American Piety: The Nature of Religious Commitment* (Berkeley: University of California Press, 1968).

figure in a most improbable place—in the underground establishment and in the headshops that have emerged as the Sears Roebuck of the youth counter-culture. Posters proliferated, advertising Jesus as a hippie, capitalizing on the length of his hair, and marketing his radical political ideologies. The youth counter-culture was sold on Jesus.

After a period of a few years, Jesus settled in as the traditional American antihero. The antihero tends to be a figure who (1) is opposed to the law, which is seen as the corrupt tool of those who wish to protect vested interests, (2) is a friend to the poor and gives generously to them out of a sense of justice, (3) is inclined to subscribe to orthodox religion, (4) adopts the role of a "trickster" vis-à-vis the authorities, and (5) tends to be subject to betrayal by friends.[4] Conformity to these characteristics placed the historical Jesus at the center of the youth counter-culture. As with most cult heroes, Jesus was called upon both to symbolize and to legitimize the emerging youth counter-culture.

Jesus' rise to prominence among the young in such a short span of time surely qualifies him for the label that Andy Warhol reserved for cult heroes—a Superstar. Looking back, it is ironic that John Lennon's assertion about the Beatles was reversed in so short a time. Jesus is again more popular than the Beatles.

Like the Beatles, Jesus' appeal has not been restricted to the youth counter-culture. The movement has developed corollary expressions with the emergence of "Jesus people," with a strong fundamentalist ideology, and of "Jesus freaks," who have a strong antidrug ideology.

Although each of these movements is characteristically located among the young, they differ in their levels of intensity and commitment to Jesus and their ideology regarding him. "Jesus people" believe him to be clearly the deity who acts in their daily existence through miracles, while "Jesus freaks" see him as one of the first and purest examples of the antihero—the hero as loser or the hero as a regular guy, just like all of us. The point is that all the young who have turned on to Jesus have not done so for the same reasons.

4. Kent L. Steckmesser, "Robin Hood and the American Outlaw," in *Journal of American Folklore*, 79, 348–54.

WHY THE MOVEMENT AT
THIS TIME: THE
CONCOMITANT CONDITIONS

Social scientists have found evidence for a religious revival having occurred in the 1950s.[5] The current interest in Jesus, however, differs from the revival of the '50s, and the major difference seems to be that the present revival is taking place primarily outside the churches.

The current revival differs from that of the '50s as much as a Brahms symphony differs from a rock festival, or as the Four Freshmen differ from the Grateful Dead. The religious revival of the '50s was a revival of institutional religion, whereas the recent "Jesus revival" is contrary to institutional religion and perhaps even antagonistic toward it. The Jesus generation holds beliefs similar to those of other Christians, but they practice these beliefs and experience the person of Jesus more enthusiastically and ecstatically than members of the traditional churches. The depth of their antagonism is, therefore, not related to the dogma of mainline denominations but to their bureaucratic organization. The churches in America have become outstanding examples of bureaucracy,[6] and the values of bureaucracy are diametrically opposed to the primary values of these young people.

However, the relationship between youth and the traditional churches is more complex. Both religious revivals coincide with particular points in the life cycle of these young people. Nash and Berger[7] suggest that the swelling of the church rolls in the '50s was due to an influx of children of primary-school age. Parents became affiliated with the institutional church for a variety of reasons. Some

5. Charles Y. Glock, "The Religious Revival in America," in *Religion and the Face of America* (Berkeley: University of California Press, 1959); Seymour M. Lipset, "What Religious Revival?" in *Columbia University Forum*, 2 (1959), 17–21.

6. Gibson Winter, "Religious Organization," in W. Lloyd Warner, ed., *The Emergent American Society*, I: *Large-Scale Organizations* (New Haven: Yale University Press, 1967).

7. Dennison Nash and Peter Berger, "The Child, the Family, and the 'Religious Revival' in Suburbia," in *Journal for the Scientific Study of Religion*, 1 (1962), 85–93. See also Dennison Nash, "A Little Child Shall Lead Them: A Statistical Test of an Hypothesis that Children Were the Source of the American Religious Revival," in *Journal for the Scientific Study of Religion*, 7, no. 2 (1968), 238–40.

desired to see their children receive moral training; some wanted to escape the problems of urban public schools; others wished to see their children get a higher quality, parochial-school education. In effect, a large group of postwar babies led their parents to church.

If the first of the recent religious revivals was due to children "dropping in" to the churches, the most recent revival began at the time the same statistical cohort of children began to "drop out" of bureaucratic religion and to "turn on" to alternate interpretive schemes. The ideals of organized religion and many of its concepts and values gave impetus to this search for meaning.

The antagonism of youth toward bureaucracy and their impact on demographic changes are not causal factors, however, but rather concomitant conditions of the development of the Jesus generation. Ironically, still another conditioning factor in the movement toward new religious interpretations is the church-initiated ecumenical movement. The ecumenical movement's explicit purpose is to unify the churches. Instead, ecumenism has tacitly given all religious movements equal claim to legitimation. It has resulted in an expanded religious "marketplace," with new religious expressions taken as seriously as traditional religious forms.

The consequences of increasing bureaucratization and demographic changes on an expanded religious marketplace were felt not only in denominational religion but also in civil religion in the United States. According to Robert Bellah civil religion in the United States is a well-institutionalized set of public beliefs and rituals that are held in common by most Americans.[8] In this consensual religion, George Washington is revered as our Moses, the man who finally led us out of captivity and established us as a people with a manifest destiny. The civil religion had its scriptures concretized in the Bill of Rights and the Constitution. It had its scribes in the members of the Supreme Court. It had its savior—the man who died to preserve its integrity and to redeem it with his blood—in the person of Abraham Lincoln. Consequently, civil religion, or the religion of democracy, led this nation to carry out its foreign policy with missionary zeal. Beyond their denominational affiliations, this was the syncretic but common religion that held Americans together, that integrated American society, and that over a period of four centuries inextricably bound American religion with the democratic state.

8. Robert N. Bellah, "Civil Religion in America," in *Daedalus*, 96, no. 1 (1967), 1–22.

The first indication of the breakdown of civil religion occurred early in the last decade, when many young people severed ties with their churches in order to invest their energies in the Southern civil rights movement. Perhaps most characteristic of the civil rights movement in the South was the religious motif of redemptive suffering. It was expressed in the strategy of nonviolence. Closely allied with nonviolence were two other religious themes, communalism and asceticism. The final religious themes that attracted young people to the civil rights movement were the ideas of prophetic authority and transcendence. These themes are, of course, intertwined with and derived from the concept of redemptive suffering. Those who suffer unjustly will ultimately transcend this suffering and be rewarded with victory. However, the movement that began as a sacred movement in the South secularized when it came North and finally died in the ashes of Watts.

Yet out of the civil rights experience a new, radical white movement based on the college campus arose. The ties between the leadership of SDS and the civil rights movements, especially SNCC, are clear. However, this movement offered the young not an expressly sacred movement but a movement based on secular morality. Newfield suggests that when SDSers are posed with a possible strategy they ask themselves not, "Is it workable?" or "How much support can we get on this from the liberals?" They ask themselves, "Is it right to do this?" [9] It was this moral idealism, especially when it was tied to the war in Vietnam, that held appeal to many middle-class, white young people. Nevertheless, that appeal was lost when it became obvious that SDS offered only a free-floating morality, with no sense of transcendent mission.

These movements, which attracted the energy of many young people, were merely the precursors of the breakdown of civil religion. The final bifurcation of civil religion occurred more dramatically as the Vietnam War became an increasingly divisive force. The consensual values of American civil religion were created in the context of two wars, but they broke down during the third. The Vietnam War fragmented them so that rationally stated religious views about identity, destiny, and nation were not to be found. Nevertheless,

9. Jack Newfield, A *Prophetic Minority* (New York: Signet Books, 1966). See also Harvey Cox, "The New Breed in American Churches: Sources of Social Activism in American Religion," in *Daedalus*, 96, no. 1 (1967), 135–50.

the need for religious views still prevailed among the young. They had dropped out of denominational religion (or at least were not committed to it), had seen the civil religion that President Kennedy had spoken so eloquently for in his Inaugural Address shattered in Dallas and DaNang, and so turned to alternate schemes of meaning, symbols, and rituals in an effort to achieve a sense of transcendence.

The young were greatly in need of some unifying experience, some deeply felt focus for their lives. As a result, many turned to drugs and rock music. These experiences were sought by the young because they added new dimensions to their lives and put ordinary experience in a different perspective. Yet the drug ethos—the shared symbols, rituals, communal feelings—was a religious phenomenon without reference to a super-empirical deity. It sought transcendence in the inner dimensions of the self.

Rock music supplies the occasion for the ritualistic celebration of this expression of the inner-self as well as for a new social ethos. A rock festival is a celebration of a communal life and epitomizes egalitarianism. Drugs and rock music supply a means of identification, a vehicle for finding meaning, and an impetus for living out a transcendent sense of reality.

While each of these movements wanders further away from traditional religion, it has been left to the Jesus movement to fashion the values of each of these alternative schemes into a quasi-traditional religious movement. Having examined some of the sources of the Jesus movement, let us now turn to its dimensions.

WHO JOINS THE MOVEMENT: THE RELIGIOUS YOUTH CULTURE

There are a large number of young people both in the churches and outside of them who endorse religious values or endorse values of the youth culture that are religious in nature. They use religious values as symbols, respond to them in their music, and think of these values as part of the discovery being made by young people.

Berger's discussion of the "youth movement" is particularly useful in analyzing this religious movement. He distinguishes between three related but distinct concepts—youth culture, youth movement, and radical movements.[10] These concepts can be thought of as concentric circles, each smaller than the preceding one.

Youth culture is the broadest of these phenomena. It is found in all advanced industrial societies and has its roots in the composition of the populations of these societies. It finds its most consistent expressions in music, the media, clothes, and the use of soft drugs such as marijuana.

The second entity, that of youth movements, represents an ad hoc activation of the youth culture around certain issues or values that are salient to some of its members. Youth movements require more of a commitment on the part of their members. They are goal oriented, but use legitimate means, and are characteristically political in nature, although politics is not endemic to such movements. The "Children's Crusade" of Senator McCarthy in 1968 would be an example of the youth movement.

The third entity, that of radical movements, is at the moment in a state of tenuous symbiosis with the broader youth context. It of course demands a higher level of commitment than the other levels of the youth movement, involves fewer individuals, and is goal oriented, but its tactics are considered less than legitimate by most of those in the broader youth context. The Weathermen faction of SDS would be an example of the radical youth movement.

The Religious Youth Culture

The extent of the religious motif in the youth culture is evidenced by the number of rock musicians who have incorporated faith rock in their recordings. The list includes: Judy Collins (*Amazing Grace*); Spirit in the Flesh (*Spirit in the Flesh*); Cat Stevens (*Tea for the Tillerman*); The Who (*Tommy*); Moody Blues (all albums); Country Joe McDonald (*Hold On It's Coming*); Kris Kristofferson (*The Silver Tongued Devil and I*); Bob Dylan (*New Morning*); Jethro Tull (*Aqualung*); George Harrison (*All Things Must Pass*); Donovan (*Wear Your Love Like Heaven*); Johnny Cash (*The Holy Land*); and the Beatles (*Sergeant Pepper* and *Magical Mystery Tour*). Eastern religious rock is represented by George Harrison, Swami Satchidananda, Pharoah Sanders (*Karma*), and the Radha Krishna Temple. Occult rock is represented by La Lupe, Mick Jagger, and Black Sabbath.

10. Peter L. Berger and Richard J. Neuhaus, *Movement and Revolution* (Garden City, New York: Anchor Books, 1970).

It is difficult to discern whether this music created a culture responsive to religious themes or whether the religious interests of the culture enabled the groups to express these themes in the most significant medium of youth—their music. However, this music does reveal the values placed on ecstasy in youth culture and correspondingly the devaluation of science, technology, rationality, totalistic theories, and bureaucracy.[11]

The religious values of the youth culture have also been demonstrated in two New York stage productions, *Jesus Christ Superstar* and *Godspell*—both musicals, both centered about the gospel narratives of the life of Jesus, and both enormous successes. This, of course, is not the first time God has starred on Broadway (*Green Pastures*, 1930; *J.B.*, 1956; and *Gideon*, 1961), but previously He had been cast in fairly traditional Godly roles.

In his most recent appearances Jesus takes on other dimensions. *Godspell* represents the fun-and-games interpretation of religion. It features a clown in patchwork overalls (Harvey Cox—*Feast of Fools*) who bears little resemblance to the Jesus portrayed in the gospel. Nevertheless, He and His followers remind one of Ken Kesey and his Merry Pranksters (*The Electric Kool Aid Acid Test*) and they do entertain, with their pratfalls, pure energy, and vaudevillean charm.

The second coming on Broadway (the best-publicized ever) was *Jesus Christ Superstar*. Here, with the help of Tom O'Horgan (*Hair*), we have God at his gaudiest, making his entrance in a monumental silver cape, singing saccharine songs of peace and love.

But in the end, questions of aesthetic merit and theological verity do not explain the importance or success of these musicals. The explanation is found in understanding their social purpose. The composition of the audiences seems to indicate that these productions are a means of reducing the chasm between the young and the middle-aged. No doubt both groups filter the experience through their own perspectives while hoping it is something to be shared. Parents feel that toying with religion is at least less noxious an opiate than methamphetamine. In addition, these productions provide for the possibility of a ritualistic celebration (an indoor Woodstock Festival) of the values of the Woodstock Nation. They affirm the solidarity of

11. Theodore Roszak, *The Making of the Counter Culture* (New York: Doubleday, 1969); Charles Reich, *The Greening of America* (New York: Random House, Inc., 1970); and Philip Slater, *In Pursuit of Loneliness: American Culture at the Breaking Point* (Boston: The Beacon Press, 1970).

the young, legitimize their values, and serve as a means of recruitment to these values.

The values that these musicals espouse are humanistic and personalistic ones such as sensitivity, responsiveness, openness, sensualism, ecstasy, communal solidarity, peace, antimaterialism, and radical egalitarianism (which explains their emphasis on the humanity of Jesus). All of those values were nascent in previous youth movements and emerged in response to the continuing problem of bureaucratic rationalism—an ethos of emphatic impersonality. However, the recent trend in music and the stage productions involving Jesus have provided a context for the articulation of the values of the new humanism as well as a context within which young people may become seriously interested in religious transcendence. They precipitate, or at least facilitate, the development of religious movements. The broad youth culture has permitted a quiet interest in Jesus, yoga, meditation, Hare Krishna, Meher Baba, astrology, and the use of drugs for the purpose of transcendent experience.

The Religious Youth Movement

The second entity, which draws its membership from the first, is that of religious youth movements. The religious youth movements centered on the person of Jesus can be somewhat arbitrarily divided into those of "Jesus people" and those of "Jesus freaks." Jesus people are the current members of campus organizations whose existence predates the renewed interest of the Jesus generation. Such organizations as the Campus Crusade for Christ and Navigators, whose membership files were embarrassingly empty only five years ago, are now exhibiting new vigor. The revival of such organizations seems to indicate a symbiotic or possibly parasitical relationship between them and the media exposure of the Jesus freaks. In contrast to "Jesus people," "Jesus freaks" are more allied with the values of the youth culture and less allied with the values of the mainline churches.

However, "Jesus freaks" do not totally endorse all the values of the youth culture. What distinguishes this group is that the individual member has committed himself to the goal of the movement but usually has not done so on a full-time basis or has not organized around that goal.

Some aspects of the "Jesus freak" movement illustrate this level of analysis. It is an amorphous movement with its own symbols (One Way!), rituals (free concerts, with an invitation to accept Jesus), newspaper (*Hollywood Free Paper*) and musicians (J. C. Power Outlet and Love Song). It is composed of two age groups. The first is a fringe group of "Jesus boppers"—white, middle-class teenagers who perhaps find the movement a temporary solution to problems of the psychosexual identity crisis characteristic of early adolescence.[12] The second group is a smaller, more intense group of young adults who reportedly have extensive experience in the drug culture. For these the Jesus movement is often a ritual of reentry into the system from which they previously dropped out. Both groups are fundamentalist, authoritarian, revivalistic, antiintellectual, antirational, and politically conservative. Their values are similar to those of the youth cultures in some respects, but differ in other respects. "Jesus freaks" espouse personalistic values, ecstasy, sensitivity, responsiveness, openness, communal solidarity, and antimaterialism, which they have channeled into a religious movement. On the other hand, they reject the values of sensualism and radical egalitarianism that the youth culture has adopted.

Radical Religious Movements

The final level of the Jesus generation is that of the radical religious movements. The distinguishing characteristics of these movements are the intensity of their option for "other-worldly" values and their commitment to organize around these values. This level is comprised of autonomous religious communes, which are often not visible because they are located in rural areas and their members live an ascetic, pastoral existence that does not include proselytizing. The members are not employed outside of the commune and do not participate in the cultic aspects of the Jesus movement. Their values are similar to the personalistic values of the movement, except that they are more ascetic, disciplined, and antimaterialistic and emphasize communal solidarity to a greater extent. They also differ from the youth culture over the question of egalitarianism. At very least, they maintain the hierarchy between themselves and God.

CONCLUSION

The last decade has seen a number of youth movements, of which the Jesus generation is a partial product. Throughout this period

12. Robert Adams and Robert Fox, "Mainlining Jesus," in *Transaction*, 9, no. 4 (February 1972), 50–56.

young people have gradually fashioned a set of values that differ from those of the preceding generation. They have been engaged in a "bargaining process" between their culture and the larger society— a bargaining process that sees the young increasingly successful in achieving acceptance of their definition of reality. At this point, whether Jesus will have a meaningful place in this definition of reality or whether the majority of young people will continue to worship only themselves remains to be seen.

SGT. PEPPER, HAIR, & TOMMY: FORERUNNERS OF THE JESUS=ROCK MOVEMENT

Patrick Morrow

IT SEEMS THAT ONLY LAST YEAR THE QUESTION "IS GOD DEAD?" ENTERED everybody's coffee conversations, was an issue where bumper stickers took sides, and provided the technicolor subject that blared forth from the covers of *Newsweek* and *Time*. Attendance at churches continued to drift downwards; Pope Paul, Billy Graham, and even Bishop Pike were chided for the lack of relevance their messages had to contemporary life. Worst of all, the youth of America had expressed its profound alienation by ignoring God and organized Christian religion and turning to astrology, Tarot cards, the black arts. Such a scene is now past history. As beatniks evolved into hippies, hippies are joining with Campus Crusade for Christ and turning into Jesus freaks. The Second Coming is upon us and the Jesus revolution is here, not as some slow-thighed beast slouching towards Bethlehem, but as a new Great Awakening in the persons of millions of young Americans afire with Pentecostal passion, a whole movement that sees Jesus as both good buddy and awesome supernatural power. Arriving on the scene garbed in sandals, jeans, and tie dyed T-shirts, they see that Bible clutched in their hand as God's relevant word, and believe in "witnessing," preaching, and love. The Jesus people want to convert YOU!

One key medium young enthusiasts for Jesus use to spread the message—wherever they may be along the reactionary to radical

"*Sgt. Pepper, Hair*, and *Tommy*: Forerunners of the Jesus-Rock Movement," by Patrick Morrow. Copyright © 1973 by Patrick David Morrow. This article appears for the first time in this volume. Printed by permission of the author.

religious line—is that central cultural and artistic voice of the now generation—rock music. In the past year Jesus has moved to a position of prominence on the Top 40. Such worldly radicals as George Harrison and Joan Baez are singing "My Sweet Lord," and "Put Your Hand in the Hand." Rock groups used to assume the most sexually suggestive names they could get away with in public; now new groups go by such names as The God Squad, Jesus Pleases, Faith and Hope, Amazing Grace, and The Joyful Noise. Among the Jesus movement converts are such important popular music figures as Johnny Cash, Eric Clapton, Paul Stookey (of Peter, Paul, and Mary), Jeremy Spencer (of Fleetwood Mac), Kris Kristofferson, and Rita Coolidge. Rock operas using Jesus and Christianity as the major themes are heavily in vogue. *Joseph and the Technicolor Dreamcoat* and *Godspell* were released in 1971 and are currently being staged across the United States. A year later *Truth of Truths* opened sunrise Easter services in Griffith Park with a rock beat. *Jesus Christ Superstar* is a national sensation as a record album and Broadway musical.

Certainly one major reason for this huge Jesus revival is His legitimization to the youth culture through appearances in songs by rock artists. While Jesus' début on the rock scene seems to have happened with sudden intensity, such is really not the case. The Jesus-rock movement is less a radical new direction for popular music than the fulfillment of ideas presented in three recent major musical productions, all of which usually are considered to be dangerous and subversive antitheses to spirituality, Jesus, the Messianic calling, and Christian conversion. These three productions are, in chronological order, The Beatles' album *Sgt. Pepper's Lonely Heart's Club Band,* the American tribal love-rock musical, *Hair,* and The Who's rock opera, *Tommy.*

Think back to early 1967. That's when The Beatles were those nice young British chaps—hair a little extreme, maybe, but their albums were song collections that evolved from "I Wanna Hold Your Hand" to "Eleanor Rigby." They sang the popular line of mass alienation and noninvolved social protest from the smug standpoint of cheerful sarcasm. Even middle-class suburbanites could enjoy such fare. But *Sgt. Pepper* put The Beatles in another league. This album worked as a whole, not as a collection of numbers but as an oratorio with themes and subthemes, complete and complex in its music, forging a new direction in popular culture. On the album's cover the old Beatles, black-suited figures from Madame Tussaud's wax museum, looked over a freshly planted grave that spelled "Beatles" in red blooming nightshade, bordered by marijuana plants and other more exotic psychedelic flora. The new Beatles, near the album's center, have converted to psychedelic uniforms, and the background above their heads suggests an hallucination of their favorite people's faces. The cover is complex and allegorical, conceived as detailed realism within an unrealistic setting, a technique that was to become the hallmark of "acid art," from the ad art of Peter Max to the San Francisco psychedelic poster school. Sergeant Pepper and the band are merry trippers, beyond alienation. They promise the tuned-in listener a happy life with a circus consciousness, provided by dope.

The first side of *Sgt. Pepper* has a consistent theme—the joy of turning on to drugs. Dope helps you cope, as the song "Getting Better" suggests, with its catalogue of violent actions and resentments that the singer claims to have recently overcome. "A Little Help from My Friends" has an orientation toward getting "high" with love, friendship, and community. A new consciousness produces a new self, thus the integrity of being on your own trip. The enjoyment of nonverbal euphoria by oneself and with other drug converts continues in "Fixing a Hole," a song that also suggests the possibility of finding a worthwhile identity through using drugs. Hallucinatory experience transferred to the music medium is one of The Beatles' great achievements in *Sgt. Pepper*. "Lucy in the Sky with Diamonds" —we note the L.S.D. initials—is about meeting your girl on an acid trip, John Lennon's claims of innocence to the contrary. Drinking milk or Geritol just does not produce in one's head the scintillating visionary imagery that appears in this song. Such wildly improbable figures as the rocking-horse people and plasticine porters indicate life in another dimension. "Being for the Benefit of Mr. Kite" extends this trip even further, with ultra-loud sounds and an astounding instrumentation, including steam calliope, synthesizers, and echo chambers.

The first cut on side two, "Within You, Without You," extends the drug consciousness from an experiential realm to a scene of intellectual meditation with Eastern ying and yang questions, sitars, and meditative mood. The talk of filling up one's mental space by seeing the vision of a new world of love (". . . if they only knew") again defines the drug scene. This song moves from everyday consciousness into a spiritual dimension. The lines that tell the listener of the peace of mind to be found when he has seen "beyond" himself would not be at all inappropriate ad libbed in *Tommy* or even *Jesus Christ Superstar*. "Within You, Without You" is a key song in the *Sgt. Pepper* album. It defines a drug consciousness as spiritual, suggests that a loving "active passivity" can help end personal and human misery, and that dope is a sacrament to reach higher planes. This song also defines "The Enemy"—those who hide behind their illusions, those who gain the world and lose their souls. They will appear other places in this album as bureaucrats, the older generation, society, and most immediately to the record's audience—un-turned-on Mom and Dad. This secondary theme of the generation gap, heads *versus* straights, is heralded on the first side by the cut "She's Leaving Home." This song masterfully uses stereophonic sound to depict a noncommunicative ageold meaningless dialogue between parent and child.

Wallowing in self-pity and materialism, Mom and Dad never understand why daughter leaves with the mysterious gigolo from the motor trade. Blind to truth in "She's Leaving Home," the Old Folks are pathetic and absurd in "When I'm 64." The wailing clarinet suggests the hopelessness of age, as these Laborite folks turn into dehumanized victims of socialism, telling at the last of their antique, dried up love by filling in a blank. In "Good Morning, Good Morning" meaningless ritual occupies the mental space of people who every morning wake up dead. Possibly the best song, musically and thematically, in the album is the finalé, "A Day in the Life." Here conversion to spirituality through a drug consciousness is posed as an alternative to participation in a grotesque society where people blow out their brains from boredom after failing to remember what was supposed to be their purpose in life.

Sgt. Pepper is manifesto and how-to album, an explicit guide to turning on the spiritual dimension in one's self with dope and dropping out of a society visualized as absurd and insane. *Sgt. Pepper* sets the stage for two possible responses. One can follow drugs into daemonic metaphysics, as does His Satanic Majesty, Mick Jagger and The Rolling Stones. A group such as Black Sabbath also follows this path. Or, one can take a sense of drug-oriented spirituality into Christian territory, as *Hair* does. *Hair* is what happens when turning on becomes a teenage life-style; it is the story of an entire counter-culture's habits and mores. The tribe, costumed like Indians to create a sense of nostalgia, noble alienation, and romanticized doom, opposes a Fascist, collectivist society that tries to force them into fighting an insane war and prosecutes as illegal their self-styled spiritual celebrations of dope and sex. Such is *Hair*'s view of America. Emersonian self-reliance has become hip anarchism as the tribe turns away from a hostile society and toward affirmation of the self.

Sgt. Pepper satirized Mom, Dad, and Society as the enemy; *Hair* reduces them to caricature. Possibly an extension of the paying customers (and ten dollars a seat is a lot to shell out just to get dumped on), Mom and Dad confront the tribe with such questions as "When are you kids going to get jobs," or "Don't you know you're being un-American?" or—sigh and shake of head—"WHY?" Dad, complete with bald pate, Polaroid, and Babbitt mentality, wants to know "What's happening to our bedrock foundation of baths and underarm deodorant?" Mom, after telling the tribe to "be free . . . do whatever you want . . . can we get a picture of you?," turns to the audience, pulls open her coat, and with a leer reveals herself as a transvestite. Mom and Dad represent a world of progress and competition gone sour, a condition heavily criticized in *Hair*. Litanies of atrocities perpetuated by the older generation occur and recur throughout the production; society as manipulator and divestor is attacked in the song "Ain't Got No" and in several racial numbers. In "Air" Jeanie pops up from a sewer hole and, through the fog and smog, condemns pollution. "What a Piece of Work is Man" brutally and movingly contrasts the carnage of war with Hamlet's eloquent soliloquy on human potential.

In *Hair* the spiritual is often couched in terms of the physical. The most holy thing one possesses is one's body, so that physical energy comes to equal spiritual grace. Protagonist Claude Bukowski sings "I Got Life," a three-minute catalogue listing numerous parts of the body after the repeated phrase "I got." The title song, "Hair," extends the idea of the body as the only spiritual tabernacle we've got by celebrating the Hippie's crowning glory. Claude calls his hair "Biblical," wants it "long as God can grow it," and then asks the poignant question of Mom and Dad: "My hair like Jesus wore it/Hallelujah, I adore it/Hallelujah, Mary loved her son/Why don't my mother love me?" "Black Boys, White Boys" advocates sexual miscegenation as spiritually and physically "healthful," "delicious," and "nutritious." The place where you can "never sin" turns out to be the bed. The hymn "Sodomy" lists illegal sexual activities with a lyrical reverence to organ accompaniment.

Achievement of spirituality through drugs, the way of life *Sgt. Pepper* advocated, becomes dramatized in *Hair* in several long scenes. On one trip the stoned tribe demands: "How dare they [society and it laws] try to end this beauty?" And after singing of violence, bodies, and an evil society, the tribe dives into rediscovering sensation. They sing: "My Body/Is Walking in Space/My Soul is in orbit/With God face to face." There are two other important spiritual scenes in *Hair*. "Hare Krishna" became the theme song of a youthful national religious movement by the same name. During this be-in number, one of the characters strips, trying to achieve a spiritual euphoria through physical liberation, out of his mind on drugs. "Starshine," with its equating of primitive simplicity with spirituality, advocates conversion to brotherly love and uses light as the symbol for spiritual grace and truth.

While *Hair* has been banned in Wyoming and other outposts as heralding an Aquarian Age of dope, sex, vulgarity, low comedy, and antiwar feeling, the American tribal love-rock musical satirizes the hippies just as much as it satirizes Mom and Dad. The hip life style is condemned for being blindly self-centered. Most of the characters are on such intense ego trips that they constantly show an indifference, even hostility, to the desires and needs of one another. A look at the behavior of several important characters shows their lack of admirability. Crissy, an early version of the teeny-bopper groupie, sings about her love for a boy named Frank Mills, whose address (somewhere in Brooklyn) she lost. He "has gold chains on his/leather jacket/and on the back is written the names/Mary and Mom and Hell's Angels." Crissy will reappear in *Tommy* as Sally Simpson, the girl who feels incomplete and unhappy unless she can spend her hours as close to a "star" as possible, basking in his golden rays of popularity. Berger, *Hair*'s tribal leader, is hung up on maintaining a charismatic *machismo*. Often he is merely a selfish and brutal demagogue. Against his harshness and inhumanity Sheila sings "How Can People Have No Feelings?" She tells Berger, "You're like everything you're against." Far from perfection herself, Sheila believes more in social protest causes than in people. Woof, addicted to drugs and homosexuality, graphically demonstrates a weakness of Hippie solipsism—such a self-destructive life can turn into a more miserable existence than life with the enemy establishment. The tribal ideal of spirituality and togetherness is often undercut by the frequent hostilities of individual members. While the "Hare Krishna" chant and "Good Morning, Starshine" promise "peace, love, freedom, happiness," the actuality of the characters' values and behavior remains far below this ideal.

Yet, *Hair* has a hero—not Berger, the tribe's leader, but Claude, who is ambivalent about both society and the tribe. His heart belongs to the hippies, but his head is with the establishment. Claude's attempt to have a two-way life style, emphasizing doing his own thing no matter what, reaches a crisis upon receiving an induction notice from the Selective Service. Claude is torn between two worlds. He burns his library card, not his draft card, and at the tribe's antiwar rally says about the Vietnam War: "I want to be over here doing the things they're defending over there." But later Claude tells Berger, "I can't live like this any more. I'm not happy. It's too difficult, I can't open myself up like that. I can't make this moment to moment living on the streets. . . . I just want to have lots of money." Claude forsakes the tribe, gets his hair cut, and goes off to Vietnam, soon brought back in many productions of *Hair* to stage center, spotlighted, on a bier—dead.

What is so striking about Claude is the open and unabashed way in which the authors, Ragni and Rado, view him as a latterday Christ. The name Claude (clod?) Bukowski may suggest a comic Christ sprung from Polish jokes—he is much more sacrificial lamb than even reluctant Messiah—but Claude is also clearly Christ. Blond, bearded, and with flowing hair, he looks like a grammar-school holy-card Christ and near the musical's end even dresses like this familiar figure in a white, gold-embroidered, floor-length linen gown. Claude believes in man as God in the song "Manchester, England, England" and later says (quietly) "I am the Son of God." Near the end of *Hair* Claude confides to Sheila, "I come from another planet," and this other world is a pastoral place of Elysian beauty and self-realization, like the Protestant Heaven children are told about in Sunday School. Claude's claim of invisibility does not grant him exemption, however, and a corrupt, ignorant, materialistic society put him to death. The tribe, insofar as they are Claude's disciples, regard him as an admirable outsider possessing special powers, but at the end they desert him to face the Southeast Asia Golgotha alone. Berger sings about "Lookin' for Madonna" and sets Claude up with a blissful night with Mary Magdalene Sheila, but ultimately Berger is no more willing to follow Claude's way than Woof, who mocks communion by saying "This is the body and blood of Jesus Christ and I'm going to eat you." Finally, according to the stage directions, there should be overhanging the whole production a permanent set piece of:

> A Crucifix-Tree—stage left center—a metal, modern sculpture Crucifix, with a rather abstract Jesus on it. . . . Jesus is electrified with tiny twinkling lights in his eyes and on his body. At times, of course, the tree is climbed.

Hair poses the great unsolved teenage question of what one can do about a lack of identity. The nude number, "Where Do I Go?," at the end of Act I, shows a far more vulnerable than erotic tribe, with their arms extended and hands stretched out, palms up. Claude, the uncomfortable Christ, sings "Where is the something/Where is the someone/That tells me why/I live and die." This search for purpose underlies a key theme of *Hair*: neither the tribal hippie street-scene nor the dying nation of moving paper fantasies is the answer to how to live a meaningful life. *Hair* sets the stage for a new way—salvation through Christian participation and emulation of Jesus. The Christ figures of Hemingway, Faulkner, Greene, Camus, Mann, and Nathanael West find that the spirituality of religion and ritual in which they cannot believe rubs off on them anyway. However parodied, mocked, or distorted, the Christian framework is a familiar one. Paradoxically, modern disillusion has prepared the way for contemporary renewal of belief. *Hair* and Claude follow the tradition and pave a new way.

Hair seems radical because of its profanity, sexual openness, anti-war protests, racial views, and satiric damning of Americanism and other traditional values. But this show is firmly rooted in the musical-comedy tradition, a successor to *South Pacific*, *My Fair Lady*, and *The Music Man*. Different tunes for different times. Musicals reflect and reinforce the overt and covert values of a given time, and *Hair*'s popularity tells us much more about the ways in which the values of millions of Americans have shifted than it shows us new developments in musical comedy. Except for the instrumental dance numbers and dope visions, *Hair* is almost compulsively straight musically. Ballads, parodies of The Supremes, love songs, protest songs—all are delivered in common time with unusually simple chords, easily adapted to the "you, too, can play along" songbooks on sale for beginning guitarists.

Tommy, on the other hand, is something else right from the beginning. This production, by an English group called The Who, led by Peter Townsend, is an opera, limited by being exclusively rock but still created in a more sophisticated form than the musical. Whether in concert or staged, this musical drama takes the audience on an amazing journey, a magical mystery tour where one number evolves into another, where a kaleidoscopic consciousness of sound creates several hours of musical hallucinations, often spiritual in content. In *Tommy,* melody, instrumentation, tempo, and mood lead the words and story; when performed on stage, the rock opera has a three-dimensional mosaic quality, often not any too coherent, where several actions happen at once. This is an amateur experiment, exciting and disjointed, emphasizing musical dramatic action, not ideas. Despite its complexity and sometimes chaos with plot, staging, and music, *Tommy* is centered on its hero: his birth, youth, success as a pinball wizard, ascendency as religious rock Messiah, and grief in isolation upon the desertion of his disciples.

Tommy encounters numerous traumatic incidents through the first part of his journey. Just before his birth near the end of World War I, Tommy's father, Captain Walker, is reported missing in action. Mrs. Walker takes a lover, but suddenly the Captain returns and kills the lover in a fit of rage. The only witness to the murder is Tommy. His parents ruthlessly brainwash him to erase his memory of the event and they succeed too well. Tommy becomes a victim of psychosomatic shock, turns deaf, dumb, and blind, and enters a world entirely in his mind. In this withdrawn and vulnerable state Tommy continues to be victimized by other characters, who are allegorical representations of a perverse and decadent society. The sadist Cousin Kevin burns Tommy with cigarettes and tries to drown him. Uncle Ernie, a drunken homosexual, uses Tommy for physical gratification. Motivated by greed and filled with malice and false promises, the gypsy Acid Queen gives Tommy LSD and sends him on a horror-filled mental trip, brilliantly depicted in the long instrumental, "Underture." Clearly Tommy's family is despicable, but so is the Acid Queen. This production, moving beyond *Sgt. Pepper* and *Hair,* suggests that drugs produce not a spiritual euphoria but an obscene nightmare and that in order to attain an enlightened, Christlike spirituality one must be converted away from drugs.

Despite his victimization, Tommy's suffering is not enough. The Who feel that Tommy needs to be saved, an idea that even dense Captain Walker recognizes in the song "Christmas." He asks:

> And Tommy doesn't even know what day it is.
> Doesn't know who Jesus was or what praying is.
> How can he be saved?
> From the eternal grave?

Tommy's physical cure, achieved in "Go to the Mirror," suggests a spiritual, saving enlightenment. In this opera truth comes in blows— much more dramatic this way—and the violence and trauma in "Go to the Mirror" and "Smash the Mirror" point to Tommy's conversion. Tommy recovers his senses as he lost them—through the violence of his parents. At the climax of the opera and its most tense moment, Tommy confronts the mirror and sees:

> A vague haze of delirium creeps up on me.
> All at once a tall stranger I suddenly see
> He's dressed in a silver sparkling
> Glittering gown
> And his golden beard flows
> Nearly down to the ground.

Tommy achieves a spiritual self-realization by recognizing that he is not alone. Rejected and tortured by society, withdrawn and plagued by self-doubts, Tommy finds God in the mirror. The figure described in the verse looks like Claude from *Hair* or the Jesus of our childhood holy-cards (with a lengthened beard to suggest a patriarchal God as well?) and acts like the Holy Spirit. In terms of touch, sound, and sight, Tommy understands:

> Listening to you I get the music
> Gazing at you I get the heat
> Following you I climb the mountain
> I get excitement at your feet!

> Right behind you I see the millions
> On you I see the glory
> From you I get opinions
> From you I get the story.

That this whole opera could be an elaborate put-on or hoax has occurred to several people, including John Lennon. But straight Christian parable, kitchy camp satire, or both, *Tommy* brings forth spirituality and an imitation of Christ as positive goals. After his faith-healing Tommy becomes a Messiah, preaching a doctrine of freedom and guided by the mysterious stranger in the long, golden robe. He says to his disciples: "If I told you what it takes/To reach the highest high/You'd laugh and say 'Nothing's that simple.'" He gains countless apostles, and builds Holiday camps (religious retreats in the woods) across the country. But Tommy demands of his followers an extreme discipline of physical deprivation and commitment to an inner spiritual sense, and the followers, finding this too difficult, revolt. The followers finally renounce Tommy in "We're Not Gonna Take It," and while he has moved beyond earthbound materialism, Tommy, at the end, is alone with his transcendent "spiritual" sense. Two other factors undercut this new Messiah. Uncle Ernie returns and promptly bungles the camp management, finally turning into a practical-joking Judas. And The Who tantalizingly introduce, without resolving it, the possibility that Tommy's spiritual solipsism has a Fascist as well as a Christian side, thus making Tommy into a character very much like Valentine Michael Smith in Robert Heinlein's *Stranger in a Strange Land.*

Virtually everyone in the opera, from Captain and Mrs. Walker to the disciples, perverts Tommy's repeated cry and song, "See me, feel me, touch me, heal me." This haunting melody, a plea for recognition and acceptance, appears throughout the opera: first in "Christmas," which contemplates Tommy's deaf, dumb, and blind condition; then in the "Underture," Tommy's drug trip; later the song becomes part of "Go to the Mirror," Tommy's cure; and in the finalé, "We're Not Gonna Take It," the cry is drawn out and repeated three times. This repetition of Tommy's song of internal self-definition and external rejection possibly shows that the suffering that Tommy endures transcends mortal pain and becomes spiritual enlightenment through the guiding force of the Godlike Mysterious Stranger.

It is an easy transition from *Tommy* to *Jesus Christ Superstar.* Both heroes spend three-fourths of their lives in obscurity and then become converted to a life of Messianic fervor, preaching the need for living a better life through spiritual enlightenment. Tommy and Jesus become Superstars, who experience adulation and glory followed by betrayal of their disciples and destruction by their own weaknesses and a malevolent society. Both works have a mood of serious purposefulness. There are, of course, some major differences between *Tommy* and *Jesus Christ Superstar*—for instance, point of view. We see Tommy as the conventional hero in the foreground position, while Jesus remains a mystery because we see him mainly through the speeches, values, and needs of others. Like Tommy, the Jesus of *Superstar* is a loner on a mission, a hero whose forebears include Odysseus, Galahad, and, more recently, Natty Bumpo, The Virginian, Tom Mix, and Shane. *Jesus Christ Superstar* takes much from *Tommy* and develops this along explicit and conventional lines. Instead of a heroic Christ figure, there is a heroic Christ; instead of an original and somewhat confusing story line, there is the familiar tale of the death of Jesus. *Tommy* depicts as an important issue the rejection of drugs as a means for achieving spiritual enlightenment. The conversion from a belief in dope to a belief in Jesus (at least for the audience) can be assumed in *Superstar*, where drugs are not an issue. But this opera arrives at a time when a young audience can accept Jesus' spirituality as real and valid because they have courted mysticism and spirituality through two mediums—drugs and religion. Tom O'Horgan's *Superstar* stage settings and costumes, by the way, owe a lot to the psychedelic and gaudy early regional productions of *Tommy*. O'Horgan's first big hit, of course, was *Hair*.

So *Godspell*, *Jesus Christ Superstar*, the new *Truth of Truths*, and many Jesus songs in the Top 40 did not become so popular without reason. The Jesus-rock movement was anticipated by three seemingly pagan, enormously popular forebears. First, The Beatles' *Sgt. Pepper* album rejected teenage alienation and nihilism by proposing living within a drug consciousness and dropping out of a mad, materialistic society. *Hair* continued an attack on the establishment, particularly Mom and Dad, but also rejected the tribal, drug-consciousness society after thoroughly exploring its possibilities. *Sgt. Pepper* presented a new way of life, but did not come forth with a hero; this *Hair* developed. Claude Bukowski was created as a kind of Christ—admirable, mysterious, reluctant, and ambivalent—who became a tragic and romantic victim. Claude dies at the end of *Hair*, so the celebratory dance is a relief to the audience (this is *supposed* to be musical comedy) because both youthful solipsism and establishment society are damned. *Tommy* also condemned a power- and money-oriented society, but concentrated on the spiritual development of its hero. Tommy's "amazing journey" went from the rejection of self, drug consciousness, and society to a realization of spiritual power through belief in a superior, external being. With its roots in the unlikliest of places, the return of Jesus as heroic and doomed superstar—the ultimate suffering and misunderstood honorary adolescent—had been prefigured these last few years by The Beatles' rock oratorio, and prophesized by Rado and Ragni's rock musical comedy, and The Who's rock opera.

CHRISTIAN COMMUNES

THE ABUNDANT LIFE FAMILY=STYLE

Ronald M. Enroth, Edward E. Ericson, Jr., & C. Breckenridge Peters

OF THE CONTRIBUTIONS THAT THE JESUS PEOPLE HAVE MADE TO American Christianity, the most interesting and most misunderstood is the Christian commune. Experiments in group living, whether religious or secular, are not new to America: New York had its Oneida; Indiana its New Harmony; North Dakota its Hutterites. But the commune has never fared well in a public opinion shaped in the mold of rugged individualism and has been particularly battered by the evangelical establishment. Pooh-poohed as the idle dream of mystic visionaries and condemned as a standing invitation to sexual orgies, the commune as a viable life style has been unhesitatingly dismissed by the church, despite the affirmations of religiosity by commune members. Yet the proliferation of Christian communes in recent years is forcing institutionalized Christianity to reevaluate its attitude.

There are several factors that contribute to the commune's slowly rising stock among America's evangelicals. First, the sincerity of belief of residents of the movement's communal houses, or at least most of them, is increasingly clear. Deciding to join a commune is a much deeper commitment than pinning on a One Way button. Communes lack the faddishness of much of the revolution. Second,

"Christian Communes: The Abundant Life Family-Style." From *The Jesus People: Old Time Religion in the Age of Aquarius*, by Ronald M. Enroth, Edward E. Ericson, Jr., and C. Breckenridge Peters (Grand Rapids, Michigan: William B. Eerdmans Publishing Company, 1972), pp. 207–20. Copyright © 1972 by William B. Eerdmans Publishing Company. Reprinted by permission of the publisher.

the communes of Jesus People do not manifest the sexual aberrations often thought to be synonymous with group living, nor are they just Christian substitutes for the drug culture. With the exception of Leon's nomadic excursions into promiscuity [Chap. 2], the communal aspect of the movement is free of both harlots and hashish. Finally, the establishment itself is beginning to involve itself in communal living to a certain degree. Church-sponsored crash pads—in reality nothing more than contemporary extensions of skid-row rescue missions—are appearing in cities throughout the United States. Though not communal in any real sense of the word, the effort has at least demonstrated that the younger generation, long hair and all, is not as licentious as had long been proclaimed. There are also some more genuine communal situations in institutional Christianity. David Wilkerson's Teen Challenge is operating a number of what can be called communal houses in its program of drug rehabilitation. While church-run houses may lack certain characteristics of full-fledged Jesus communes, the church's timid experiments in group living have stirred the realization that Christianity and the commune are not necessarily antithetical.

The movement's growing fascination with the commune is much deeper than the church's, and the revolution's experiments have produced results unheard of, and generally undesired, in more organized Christianity. The most obviously revolutionary communes are the flourishing communities established and maintained by the Children of God and Tony and Susan Alamo. Their group living is unmistakably related to their religious idiosyncrasies, which fence them off markedly from the church and, to a lesser extent, the rest of the movement. The Saugus community and the widely dispersed colonies of the Children differ from each other in some details about the holiness practices necessary to Christian living—an obvious example: the strict sexual segregation of the Alamos' Foundation, which is far more rigid than the more relaxed, though not unrestricted, relations existing in the Children's colonies. But the two are united in purpose. Unlike establishment efforts, these communities do not view themselves as temporary groupings designed to promote spiritual growth or as Christian hotels to travelers of this world. Rather, the Children and the Foundation see the commune as a new and permanent life style for America's true believers.

"New" is a bit inaccurate when applied to the communal doctrine of the Children of God. The Children themselves deny that the commune is new to Christian experience; rather, for them the terms are synonymous. Since the time of Pentecost those few Christians untainted by the demonic influence of the corrupt church have lived communally. Like the rest of the Children's dogma, the proof of the commune is in the proof-texting. Acts 2:44–45 provides the foundation, and the sincerity of the Children's efforts to abide by the supposed command is obvious. The colonies are truly communal; possessions, including even such things as clothes, are group property, and activity is seldom oriented toward the individual. Money, except in the hands of an elder, is unheard of. The colony provides all, just as it asks all. For the Children the colonies are foolproof insurance against being absorbed by the worldly system that turned the Bride of Christ into the Whore of Babylon.

The efforts of the Children to sever Christianity's long-standing ties with secular culture are certainly not half-hearted. They are striving, with slowly increasing success, to achieve complete self-sufficiency, a goal rooted in the expectation that the Antichrist and his reign of terror will not be long in coming. The future of the colonies is not often discussed, but when it is, the vision seldom stops at a network of relatively small communes spread throughout the nation. In the words of an elder, Abraham, the Children dream of "whole cities of Christians" totally apart from the society of Antichrist. The apocalypse and its accompanying disasters, coupled with the Children's post-tribulationism, make self-sufficiency imperative if they are to avoid compromising with a world order under the Mark of the Beast. Josiah, chief elder of the Children's eastern Kentucky farm, says: "We feel we've got to become self-sufficient, you see, because things are going to get worse in this country. All the things that are prophesied in the Bible are coming to pass—wars and rumors of war, nation rising against nation, all this trouble with insects and pollution."

Besides insulating disciples from the contaminating world, an equally crucial function of the colony is social control. The lack of privacy, the hierarchical power structure, the strict, no-questions-asked regime—all . . . make the colonial structure quite stable. The attrition rate is low, and most of those who do desert are persuaded by relatives, distraught pastors, and indignant friends, not by their own inclination. Colonial authority resides, totally and without question, in the local elder. Assumed to be imbued with the authority of God himself, the elder's word is law, and the disciple's submission to it is total.

The differences between the Children and the Christian Foundation clearly stem from the presence of Tony and Susan Alamo. Their justification for the communal situation existing in Saugus does not include the Acts proof-text, nor does one hear from them the clarion call to forsake all, though Foundation residents have given up most. The Alamos, rather, root their commune totally in the expected horrors of the impending Tribulation. Alamo fully expects the Foundation to retreat from the edge of the city to the mountains and eventually envisions a martyrdom for himself and his disciples under the bullets of the Antichrist, though the wounds will hurt "no more than cigarette burns."

Another parting of the ways—a theoretical one to be sure—is the Alamos' avowed intention to produce a new clergy to win the world before the end. Tony Alamo speaks of the Foundation in this sense as a temporary training ground. On the other hand, he admits that no one has yet left Saugus for the world and that he expects the apocalypse to be ready before his disciples are. Alamo claims that the Foundation is a training center, but his actions prove it to be a full-time, permanent house. Separation from the world is less rigorous at the Foundation, the main breach in security being the good-sized influx of regular visitors for Susan Alamo's services. Her husband was quite willing to lead us on a grand tour of the main meeting hall, but he flatly refused to show off the Foundation's living quarters.

The Alamos are unquestioned and generally unavailable; still, their word, conceived by Susan and repeated by Tony, is revered law. The Foundation should survive the slings and arrows of the future, at least as long as the Alamos do. But unlike the Children, who continually cultivate elders in spite of their expectation of the end, the Foundation has no such insurance scheme. The colonies of the Children could probably survive even a deferment of the apocalypse. It is unlikely that the Foundation could outlive its patron saints.

The authoritarian communal structure of the Children and the Foundation is duplicated in other scattered communities throughout the movement, but it would be incorrect to assume that only the more fanatical, totalitarian, cultic manifestations of the revolution delve seriously into the world of communal living. Significant efforts at establishing Christian communes are sprinkled throughout the move-

ment. These communities are, for the most part, designed as training
schools where believers can mature and gain firm grounding in
Scripture and Christian living before returning to the secular city.
The practical value of the commune as perceived by the Jesus People
is enunciated by the elder of the House of Emmaus in Toronto:

> People's experience has become impersonal, too abstract, and thus
> impractical. Communal living creates situations which keep your
> experience on a level of reality. That is, you may get into situations
> where you are confronted with the fact that you need more love,
> patience, humility, forgiveness towards a brother and you have to
> go to God continually for help in changing yourself. You must, so
> you do.

The communal idealism, while not realized in every instance,
is not an exercise in spiritual wishful thinking. A good example of
the merits of the movement's communes can be found in a collection
of thriving houses in and around Pasadena, California. "Our Father's
Family," as the members of the old, rambling house in a residential
section of Pasadena call themselves, began through the efforts of
two young converts, Paul Danchik and Don Pauly. (Pauly has since
moved to Florida, leaving Danchik to manage the Pasadena House.)
The house and its members are much more open and cordial than
either the Children of God or the Alamos and their disciples. The
property has several smaller dwellings in addition to the main house
and includes vegetable gardens. The smaller buildings are occupied
by Danchik and his wife Nina, along with the family of another
elder, and are furnished quite starkly. The simplicity of the elders'
quarters matches that of the large house, which accomodates the co-ed
population of about thirty. House regulations govern the times for
rising and breakfast and require residents to inform the elder of their
whereabouts, to participate in communal activities, and to contribute
to the house's treasury.

The Pasadena House screens prospective residents to keep out
those unwilling or unready to accept the life style. Most of the Family
come from permissive and unstructured backgrounds, and many have
dabbled in drugs, though heavy experimentation seems to have been
rare. New residents give up neither their possessions nor their jobs.
Indeed, each of the male residents is employed—some in structured
situations, others as free-lance gardeners—and contributes a share
(sometimes more than ninety percent) of his income to maintaining

the commune. The women are responsible for upkeep of the house and meals, and occasionally take baby-sitting jobs. Few if any of the Family attend college, simply because, in Danchik's words, "They just aren't the kind of people who are interested in that sort of thing."

Theologically the Family has, almost by trial and error, managed a charismatic but well-balanced structure. Danchik readily admits to both doctrinal and practical mistakes in the commune's development. There were stages of fixation during which the House's fascination with various aspects of the Christian life, especially the charismatic gifts and the power of exorcism, excluded other, less spectacular issues. At each stage, diligent Bible study has served as a corrective, and a balanced theology has replaced the narrow fascination by a broader appreciation. The process has been worked out by maturing believers. Danchik, converted just three years ago, is now collected, personable, and disarmingly sincere.

The House has had remarkably little aid from either established churches or other Jesus People and continues to remain a quite isolated group. Residents do occasionally attend institutionalized worship services, usually in small groups. Danchik knows of the Jesus Movement only through the media. The House shares many of the movement's dogmas—the charismatic experience and the nearness of the apocalypse are common to both—but lacks the preachy, button-holing quality of many spiritual revolutionaries. Danchik himself thinks that the term Jesus People profanes the name of Jesus. Instead, he regards the Family as "children of God" (in the nonrevolutionary sense of the term). The communal operation in Pasadena surely deserves that title.

Another highly successful communal chain, numerically at least, known as the Shiloh Houses, includes thirty-seven settlements from Oregon (where it started) to the Eastern seaboard. The first Shiloh House was established in the countryside near Eugene by John Higgins, an associate of Lonnie Frisbee in the movement's early days. Since then the commune has grown steadily, and the original Shiloh community now has a school and farm. Its doctrinal position is somewhere between the balanced theology of Our Father's Family and the more exotic dogmas of full-fledged revolutionaries. Like many communal groups, Shiloh disavows the Jesus People label, saying that the movement is too shallow to survive. Shiloh's leaders laud the commune's commitment and claim that this attribute will make their ministry a lasting one. Again, these communes share the typical characteristics of the charismatic gifts, the apocalyptic mentality, and strains of anti-intellectualism.

The three Shiloh Houses in Denver are typical of the association's communal style. Under the direction of Pastor George and his assistant, Deacon Lyle, one house is occupied by males, one by females, and another by married couples and the overflow from the male house. Life is somewhat regimented; curfew is at 11:00 p.m. Bible studies are held nightly with the exception of Sunday. The houses are open to crashers, and most residents are willing to venture into the outside world for occasional employment, but only at positions where small groups of Shiloh's members can labor together. The commune's emphasis is on personal evangelism, a concern spurred by the conviction that the apocalypse is just around the corner.

Both the hyper-evangelism and intense apocalypticism of Shiloh prevent it from cultivating the maturity shown in Pasadena. Still, Shiloh is quite removed from the cultishness of the Alamos and the Children. The middling ground occupied by Shiloh is attractive (witness the chain's thirty-seven outposts) and apparently the communes are sufficiently stable to prevent any of the branches from withering on the vine. Newsletters and training teams from the Oregon headquarters knit the communities together in a union far more professional—a trained bookkeeper is listed among the headquarters' residents—than most of the movement's fledgling associations. The Shiloh Houses continue to grow both in number and in stability. The chain is evidence that the movement's experimentation with communes is more than a wide-eyed fascination with the storied counter-culture. Rather, it is a growing attempt to establish a life style that is uniquely Christian.

Most of the movement's efforts at communal living have met with neither the success of Shiloh nor the maturity of the Pasadena House. More typical is the Koinonia Community of Santa Cruz, California, founded by Mrs. Margaret Rovick, a fundamentalistic Methodist turned revolutionary. Mrs. Rovick is generally unavailable for interviews. The community began in 1967 as a simple coffee house ministry and went communal in November 1968. It has since added a restaurant, boutique, and bookstore (of sorts). The group now has two communal houses.

Some of Koinonia's twenty or so members resent any insinuation that Mrs. Rovick is the leader of the group. They claim that all members are equal and that Mrs. Rovick is just another member, though they admit that chronologically she was the first. Nevertheless, the commune residents are described by outsiders in the Santa Cruz area as "automatons" who function at Mrs. Rovick's beck and call. A decided majority of the members are female. Most residents are "reformed" street people. Koinonia also provides a home for several youthful probationers assigned to Margaret Rovick by nearby counties.

Koinonia has no regularly scheduled worship services or Bible studies. Occasionally, the group puts on a folk mass, one of the few elements from established churches that they deem worthy of imitation. Koinonia's revulsion from institutional churches is marked: "Emphatically we are not a church, and therefore refuse to get involved in doctrinal hassles." The lack of structured spiritual exercises seems strangely inconsistent with the regimentation found necessary for operating the community. The favorite exercise of devotion is fasting.

Like many elements of the movement, Koinonia is uncomfortable with the Jesus People label. This probably stems from their exclusivist temper: they consider themselves special in the eyes of God, and to link them with other groups would dilute their elect status. Still the Koinonia Community shares major traits of the Jesus Movement. It explores the charismatic gifts. It is violently anti-institutional. Its exclusivism is pronounced: visitors from nearby Mount Hermon Christian Conference Center have been barred from the community as representatives of Satan on the basis of a vision revealed to Mrs. Rovick.

While most of the Jesus Movement focuses on Christian love and joy, Koinonians are fascinated with the reality of Satan and the fear of God's retribution. The most interesting manifestation of their enthralment with the power of evil is their belief that Satan controls a section of Highway 17 on the way to San José which is frequently marred by accidents. The demonic control is thought to result from a number of "Satanist-hippie" colonies purported to be in the area. As members tell it, Koinonia has insured its own travel through the area by prayer and fasting and has yet to come under the demonic, accident-producing influence.

Koinonia Community takes itself very seriously. It is not a relaxed place. Visitors are welcome only if they "sincerely want to ask questions about the Christian concept of God." To underline the no-nonsense approach, one of their flyers rather pugnaciously declares, "Because we work long hours to support ourselves and because we give of all our free time to serving our fellow men, we will not encourage lazy people to hang around us in the hopes of somehow 'getting religion.' "

Mrs. Rovick and her band do not defend their life style by quoting scriptural injunctions to communal living, as do the Children of God. Nor do they view their commune as a refuge from the rapidly approaching Tribulation. The community exists in the name of expedience. Through it Margaret Rovick hopes to realize a viable pattern for Christian living. All she wants from the outside world is to be left alone.

Sadly, Koinonia and many of the movement's other experimental clusters have not been as fortunate as Our Father's Family of Pasadena. The balance of maturity and enthusiasm at the Pasadena House is the infrequent exception, not the rule. Most communes of the movement depend almost solely on themselves for leisure activities as well as interpersonal relations. They rely on the teachings of a single elder and have little meaningful contact with fellow believers. This social and theological isolation quite often produces an inbred ethnocentrism. Koinonia's brittle exclusivism, which characterizes itself as God's only outpost among the heretics of Santa Cruz County, is more extreme than most, but it is a direct result of the intellectual and spiritual walls erected at edges of the commune.

Such narrow vision is certainly not unknown in past religious movements. Much the same development happened in the pre-Christian Essene community, which preserved the Dead Sea Scrolls. Of the Essenes, Geza Vermes says, ". . . they were convinced that their beliefs and way of life conformed fully to the will of God and qualified them to claim the honor of being the only true Israel" (*The Dead Sea Scrolls in English*, p. 17). Though they were "a company of poor humble men constantly attentive to the word of God and grateful for His favors" (p. 51), Vermes acknowledges the probability "that their convictions gave rise to rigidity, bigotry, and hatred" (p. 52).

Though the name "commune" suggests an equality among the members, the fact is that most Jesus communes foster an unhealthy dependence on the local elder. The Alamos, Margaret Rovick, and the elders of the Children of God thrive on that sort of blind loyalty far more than other commune leaders, but even less rigidly structured communities create a hierarchy topped by someone whose pronouncements are not to be questioned. The isolation characteristic of the colony mitigates against the development of critical, evaluative thinking, another phenomenon discussed by Vermes:

> God had chosen to reveal knowledge and understanding of His purpose and will to their [the Essenes'] Teacher of Righteousness and to those of the Teacher's followers who trod the path laid down by him, the Way of Holiness. Only the Teacher was able to decipher the mysteries concealed in the Scriptures; consequently only those who accepted his interpretation of the written word of God could be sure of living in conformity with His desire (p. 35).

Working out one's salvation with fear and trembling is widely accepted in theory, but it is seldom practiced in the commune.

Despite the many misguided efforts, the revolution has been steadied by the commitment required in group living situations. Life at the commune is sobering. It is here that the revolution must put up or shut up. Communal living is at times exceedingly difficult both physically and psychologically. The Children of God were often hungry before manna from the hand of Fred Jordan descended; the Alamos' disciples still lead a Spartan existence; even the Pasadena House is minus the usual luxuries—including privacy—that grace the typical Christian home. Whatever the aberrations might be, the dedication of most of the movement's communal dwellers is impressive. Like the Essene community, Jesus communes are well-intentioned, sincere attempts to work out viable alternatives to establishmentarian religion. Ironically, it is precisely the unswerving, unquestioning, naive dedication of young revolutionaries that creates rigidity and its frequent handmaidens, bigotry and hatred.

Perhaps it is unjust to judge the Jesus Movement's efforts at communal living so hastily. Most are of recent origin. Many, like the Koinonia Community, have evolved from coffee houses and related sorts of undertakings and are still developing and adjusting. The Pasadena House, beginning its third year in operation, has had more time to mature than even the Alamos' Foundation. Much of the revolution's communal effort seems to have progressed toward a maturity but has, for a variety of reasons, become mired down in narrow, often cultish beliefs.

The Harvest House Ministries, Inc., of San Francisco plainly shows this retarded maturity in ways that are typical of the revolution as a whole. The corporation began as a Jesus commune named Harvest House in Haight-Ashbury. Its residents are apocalyptically and charismatically oriented; visions and dreams are commonplace.

Organizationally Harvest House differs little from other of the movement's efforts. Oliver Heath, a student at Golden Gate Baptist Seminary, supervises the operation because, according to a resident, "The Lord has given him a position of Pastor and he's the head of all these houses."

The maturity produced by the communal situation at Harvest House is best expressed in the community's production of a well-written, sometimes cogent newspaper, *The Oracle*. Once it was one of the raciest of the hip underground papers. Then its editor David Abraham was converted through Chris D'Allessandro, a Harvest House member. He promptly turned the paper over to Harvest House, and D'Allessandro is now one of the co-editors.

Replete with psychedelic drawings designed to appeal to "the San Francisco-type people," *The Oracle* expresses theological understandings far more developed than those expressed in the *Hollywood Free Paper* and its imitators:

> Has it ever struck you how extraordinary it is that the children of God can hear so much and *express* so little? . . . The reason for this lies in the *unrenewed mind*. They may have truly received the Holy Spirit but, speaking reverently, he is "locked up" in the spirit, and cannot get through the blocked channel of the mind. One reason is that many children of God do not soak themselves, so to speak, in God's thoughts. . . . You must never let the mind become "slack," or careless in its thinking, or it will soon fall prey to the watching enemy. The "mind" should never be idle, or without "grist for the mill." It must be active if it is in a normal condition.

The appreciation for the intellect bred at Harvest House is in short supply at other Jesus People strongholds and is indeed a step toward a balanced conception of the Christian life.

Harvest House has expanded to include other programs and is now incorporated as Harvest House Ministries, Inc. One of its new operations is a restaurant serving health foods, known as Vege-Hut. These efforts at outreach are far more complicated than the typical Jesus People fixation with face-to-face evangelism. The commune conducts the business of both *The Oracle* and the Vege-Hut for evangelistic rather than capitalistic reasons and sees merit in such indirect evangelism.

Still, there remains an extreme fascination with both the supernatural and the apocalypse, which lifts many of the houses' residents into an almost mystic world where even the smallest occurrences take on a cosmic explanation. Says one of Harvest House's family: "Like the last days are really here, and I believe it so strong that every second I look for Christ. Every time I see a lightning flash or street car thing out here flashing, I think it's Christ." Some in the houses seem to have developed what amounts to a martyr complex—not a willingness to suffer but a desire to do so. Harvest House's living situation is responsible for the cultivation of attitudes like these, which are hardly conducive to the well-rounded Christian world view.

Our impression is that Harvest House harbors young people who were more deeply involved in the counter-culture than most segments of the Jesus Movement. The houses have accepted many young mothers with illegitimate children. Sexual problems have not yet all been overcome. One young man we spoke to was rocking a baby who he admitted was his. The unwed mother lives in the same house. The father reluctantly admitted that his sexual activity was wrong, but added that he was not the only one who had trouble in this area. The situation, he said, was now fully under control. The leadership of Harvest House, especially Heath, seem reasonably mature; and there is good reason to hope that Harvest House will achieve a pattern of growth paralleling that of Our Father's Family.

The communal style of life adopted by a substantial portion of the Jesus People may last for a long time, whatever the attitude of church people may be. It has many potential advantages: the sense of spiritual belonging, a substitution for fatherless or otherwise deficient family units, economy in meeting material needs. But it also isolates a small group of believers from the larger household of faith, and so far this disadvantage has outweighed the potential advantages more often than not. Here, as elsewhere, the Jesus People need communication with other Christians. Brotherly acceptance of Jesus communes by outside Christians may not (and should not) lead to the demise of the houses, but it will minimize the dangerous tendency toward cultic isolationism. On the other hand, condemnation of the Jesus communes by straight Christians as Satanic, un-American, or otherwise disreputable will only build a higher wall of separation between the Jesus People and the rest of the Body of Christ. Once again, the fate of the Jesus People is not entirely in their own hands. Church Christians are going to have a lot to say about the outcome of the Jesus Revolution.

NOTES ON THE CONTRIBUTORS

RAZIEL ABELSON is a professor in the Department of Philosophy at New York University (University Heights). ALLEN GINSBERG is the world famous poet, essayist, and lecturer. MICHAEL WYSCHOGROD teaches in the Department of Philosophy at Baruch College, the City University of New York.

HARVEY COX teaches at Harvard University in the Divinity School. He is the author of two bestselling books on religion, *The Secular City* and *Feast of Fools*.

RONALD M. ENROTH is associate professor of Sociology at Westmont College, Santa Barbara, California. EDWARD E. ERICSON is chairman of the Department of English and Modern Language at Westmont College. C. BRECKENRIDGE PETERS is a graduate student in Sociology at the University of Kentucky. These three authors collaborated on the book *The Jesus People: Old Time Religion in the Age of Aquarius.*

JOHN FRITSCHER is a member of the English Department at Western Michigan University at Kalamazoo.

TIMOTHY LEARY is the "high priest" of the psychedelic movement in the United States. His books include *Psychedelic Prayers* and *High Priest.*

ARTHUR LYONS is the author of the recent book *The Second Coming: Satanism in America.*

PATRICK MORROW is an assistant professor of English at the University of Southern California. He is an ex-Jesuit seminarian and worked for several years as a professional musician.

JACOB NEEDLEMAN is professor of Philosophy and Religion at San Francisco State College. He is the author of the recent book *The New Religions.*